SURVEY OF BEST PRACTICES IN STUDENT RETENTION, 2019-20 EDITION

©2019 Primary Research Group Inc. ISBN 978-1-57440-597-2

Table of Contents

THE QUESTIONNAIRE

1. *Please list the requested contact information below.

   A. Name:
   B. Organization:
   C. Email Address:
   D. Work Title:

2. Your college is:

   A. A public college
   B. A private college

3. The full time equivalent enrollment of your college is approximately:

4. College type or Carnegie class

   A. Carnegie Class Community College
   B. Carnegie Class 4-year or MA degree granting institution
   C. A Carnegie Class PHD granting institution
   D. A Carnegie Class level 1 or level 2 research university

5. The approximate annual tuition (the sticker price prior to any aid or deductions) cost for attending your college is:

6. How much did the college spend on consulting services to aid in student retention in the past year? (exclude spending on conference which we ask about separately)

7. How much do you expect that the college will spend on consulting services to aid in student retention in the next year? (exclude spending on conference which we ask about separately)

8. Does the college have a dean or other high level administrator whose primary responsibility is to maintain or increase student retention?

   A. Yes
   B. No

9. What was the college's fall to fall retention rate for first year students in the fall 2013 to fall 2014 school year?

10. What was the college's fall to fall retention rate for part time students from fall 2018 to fall 2019?

11. What was the retention rate for the following specific kinds of students?

    A. Graduate Students
    B. Law School Students
    C. Distance Learning/Hybrid Learning Students
    D. Foreign Students
    E. Adult students over age 30 (or some reasonable equivalent)

12. For the last year for which such data is available, what percentage of students who start at the college as fall term freshmen graduate the college?

13. If you have had particular success in increasing retention rates for any specific group defined by any criteria -- race, SAT level, academic major, geographic origin, or any other criteria - explain how you achieved this success.

14. Using a scale of 1-4, rank the impact on retention of the following on student retention:

	Does not have much of an impact	Has some impact	Has a significant impact	Has a dramatic impact
Terms of student financial assistance				
Severity in Grading				
Access to tutoring services				
Changes in the Academic Reputation of the College				
Access to Academic and/or psychological counseling services				
General economic conditions				
Involvement in extra curricular activities				
Quality of residence halls and food service				

15. Approximately what percentage of students who decide to transfer out of or drop out of the college prior to graduation are interviewed by college management to find out their feelings about their experience at the college?

16. How important have exit interviews been in developing and implementing your retention strategy?

	Absolutely Invaluable	Useful	Somewhat Useful	Not really too Useful	Virtually Useless
Exit interviews for Departing Students who did not graduate					
Exit interview with Graduating Students					

17. Does the college maintain any records that enable it to pinpoint students who are not engaged in any or very few extra-curricular activities?

   A. Yes
   B. No

18. Your college's information literacy policy is best approximated by which statement:

   A. No specific information or computer literacy requirement
   B. Teaches information/computer literacy within the framework of the basic English Writing Course or other basic course.
   C. Requires a one or two credit information literacy or computer literacy course for graduation.
   D. Requires one or more three credit information literacy or computer literacy course for graduation.

19. Does the college offer childcare services for students with children?

    A. Yes
    B. No

20. How important do you consider part time employment for students and the provision of quality internships to be as a factor in student retention and have you made efforts to evaluate or improve these services at your college?

21. On a scale of 1-5 with "1" as very important and "5" as unimportant, how critical are the following student services for success in retention.

	Very Important	Important	Somewhat Important	Infrequently Important	Not Really Important
Office of Financial Aid					
Office of career services					
Academic Advising					
Learning Services/Tutoring Services					
Peer Mentoring					
Child Care Services					
Information Technology					

22. Does the college identify high risk students and then intervene at certain thresh-holds such as number of classes or assignments missed, or low grade point averages?

    A. Yes
    B. No

23. Which phrase best describes your view of your college's efforts to reach out to and help students at high risk for dropping out?

    A. We don't do enough and are not really very good at what we do.
    B. We don't do enough and our present efforts are passable at best.
    C. We make a fairly considerable effort and do as well as most.
    D. We make a great effort but without great results.
    E. We make a great effort and we have very good results.

24. How much did the college spend on tutoring for all students in the past year?

25. How much will the college spend next year on tutoring for all students?

26. Which phrase best describes your attitude towards the impact that the college tutoring program has had on student retention?

    A. I don't think that tutoring can have a big impact on retention.
    B. We need to hire more tutors, train them better, or both.
    C. We have a good tutoring program that has helped us to maintain or increase our retention levels.
    D. Our tutoring program is excellent and is a key factor in our maintenance of a higher than expected retention level.

27. Does the college have student advisory centers located in residence halls?

    A. Yes
    B. No

28. To the best of your knowledge, has the college ever hired a consultant to review or advise on the college's academic advising services?

    A. Yes
    B. No

29. What is the total annual budget, including spending for salaries, of the college's academic advising unit?

30. Over the past two years the college's financial aid has:

    A. Become much less generous
    B. Become somewhat less generous
    C. Remained about the same in real terms
    D. Become somewhat more generous
    E. Become much more generous

31. My personal feeling about tuition levels and the financial situation of our student body is that:

    A. It has become more and more difficult for our students to pay for college.
    B. The overall financial burden on our students has not changed much in recent years.
    C. Our aid programs and a strong economy have actually reduced the financial burden on our students in recent years.

32. The college's retention rate for first year students entering the second year has:

    A. Remained about the same in the past two years
    B. Increased in the past two years
    C. Decreased in the past two years

33. About what percentage of students who drop out do you believe do so primarily for economic reasons?

34. Over the next few years your best honest estimate is that:

    A. Our retention rates will probably decline.
    B. Our retention rates will probably stay about the same.
    C. Our retention rates will increase.

35. If your college has any of the following types of programs rank their retention rates relative to your main college program

	Retention Rates Much Below Traditional Programs	Retention Rates Below Traditional Programs	About the Same	Above Traditional Programs	Much Above Traditional Programs	N/A
Adult Education						
Distance Education						
Overseas Campus						

36. If you have taken any special measures to increase retention in distance learning or adult education programs share with us some or your insights below.

PARTICIPANTS LIST

Bacone College
Baylor University
Bethel University
Brandon University
Brevard College
Bridgwater State University
Cabrini University
College of Coastal Georgia
College of Engineering Texas A&M University
Cumberland University
East Stroudsburg University
Eastern Illinois University
Eastern Michigan University
Fresno Pacific University
Gallaudet University
Hannibal-LaGrange University
Harding University
Henderson State University
Judson University
Leading Informatics for Tomorrow (LiFT) Scholars Program
LIM College
Lyon College
MidAmerica Nazarene University
Morehead State University
Mountwest Community & Technical College
Northern Michigan University
Point Loma Nazarene University
Randolph-Macon College
Rocky Mountain College
Seton Hall University
St. Bonaventure University
Stockton University
SUNY Plattsburgh
Terra State Community College
University of Guelph
University of Pittsburgh at Bradford
University of Rochester
University of Tennessee at Martin
Ursuline College

Characteristics of the Sample

Your college is:

	#
A public college	21
A private college	21
Total	42

Enrollment

	#
Less than 1000	8
1000 - 2999	10
3000 - 7000	14
More than 7000	10
Total	42

College type or Carnegie class

	#
Carnegie Class 4-year or MA degree granting institution, Community College	34
Carnegie Class Research universities	8
Total	42

Tuition, $

	#
Less than 10000	12
10000 - 20999	6
21000 - 30000	13
More than 30000	11
Total	42

SUMMARY OF MAIN FINDINGS

Current Spending on Consulting Services to Aid in Student Retention

We asked: How much did the college spend (in U.S. $) on consulting services to aid in student retention in the past year?

The mean was $5,870.97, the median was $0.00, the minimum was $0.00, and the maximum was $50,000.00. Spending was mostly related to college size and type with colleges with more than 7,000 students FTE and research universities spending more than their counterparts.

Planned Spending on Consulting Services to Aid in Student Retention

We asked: How much do you expect that the college will spend (in U.S. $) on consulting services to aid in student retention in the next year?

The mean was $11,983.33, and the maximum was $125,000. The median and the minimum were both $0.00. Spending was more or less expected to double in the next year with public colleges leading the way with increased expenditure in the area. Small colleges still do not plan to spend much but medium sized colleges with from 3,000 to 7,000 students appear ready to step up spending.

Percentage of Colleges with a Chief Retention Officer

We asked: Does the college have a dean or other high level administrator whose primary responsibility is to maintain or increase student retention? Private colleges were significantly more likely than public ones to have some form of chief retention officer as 62% of the former but only 43% of the latter had one.

52.38% said yes, 45.24% said no, and 2.38% gave no answer.

The Fall to Fall Student Retention Rate Part Time for the 2018-19 Academic Year

We asked: What was the college's fall to fall retention rate for part time students from fall 2018 to fall 2019?

The mean rate was 68.86%, the median was 72%, the minimum was 33.00%, and the maximum was 89.50%.

Retention Rates for Graduate Students

We asked: What was the retention rate for the following specific kinds of students? First we asked about graduate students.

The mean retention rate for graduate students was 86.50%, the median was 90.50%, the minimum was 70.00%, and the maximum was 92.00%.

Retention Rates for Distance Learning Students

For distance learning/hybrid learning students, the mean was 68.00% and the median was 76.00%. The minimum was 30.00%, while the maximum was 90.00%.

Retention Rates for Foreign Students

For the foreign student population, the mean retention rate was 73.89%, the median was 83.00%, the minimum was 30.00%, and the maximum was 98.00%.

Retention Rates for Adult Students Over the Age of 30

For adult students over the age of 30, the mean was 63.60%, the median was 61.00%, the minimum was 45.00%, and the maximum was 99.00%.

Same School Graduation Rates for Undergraduates

We asked: For the last year for which such data is available, what percentage of students who start at the college as fall term freshmen graduate the college?

The mean was 55.12%, and the median was 56.00%. The minimum rate was 18.00%, and the maximum was 87.00%. The rate was much lower for public than private colleges, 48.77% for the former; 60.46% for the latter. Research and doctoral institutions did better than average, with a mean of 68.27%. As tuition rates rose, so did same school graduation rates.

Special Retention Efforts

Many survey participants noted success with programs aimed at particular groups such as students with disabilities, freshmen or ethnic or racial minority groups.

Impact of Financial Aid on Student Retention

Using a scale of 1-4, rank the impact on retention of the following on student retention:

42.86% said financial assistance has dramatic impact on student retention, and 33.33% said it has significant impact. 23.81% said it has some impact, while 0.00% said it does not have much of an impact, and 0.00% gave no answer. Close to half of private colleges felt that access to financial aid has a dramatic impact on retention rates as did 75% of colleges with enrollment of less than 1,000 students.

Impact of Severity in Grading on Student Retention

50.00% reported that severity in grading has some impact on student retention. 26.19% claimed it has a significant impact, and 19.05% said it does not have much of an impact. 2.38% said it has a dramatic impact, and the same percentage gave no answer.

Impact of Access to Tutoring on Student Retention

Access to tutoring services had a significant impact on retention, according to 57.14% of all respondents. 33.33% said that this access had some impact. 7.14% said that this access does not have much of an impact, 2.38% gave no answer, and 0.00% said that it has a dramatic impact.

Impact on Retention of Changes in the Academic Reputation of the College

Only about 4.76% overall felt that this had had a dramatic impact on retention while another 11.9% felt that it had a significant impact. For private colleges this was a greater consideration than for public ones as nearly 30% of private colleges felt that changes in their college's reputation had had an impact on retention while only 4.76% of public colleges felt the same way.

Impact on Retention of Academic and/or Psychological Counseling Services

Academic and Psychological counselling was considered to have a significant or dramatic impact by nearly 70% of survey participants. This was perhaps especially the case at research-oriented institutions where more than 87% considered it important as a factor in retention.

Impact of General Economic Conditions on Student Retention

General economic conditions were thought to have a significant impact on retention by 35.71% of survey participants and a dramatic impact by 26.19%. This impact was particularly felt by public colleges: more than 76% said it had a significant or dramatic impact on student retention.

Percentage of Dropouts or Transferees Interviewed by the College of Departure

We asked: Approximately what percentage of students who decide to transfer out of or drop out of the college prior to graduation are interviewed by college management to find out their feelings about their experience at the college?

The mean was 46.16% and the median was 50.00%. The maximum was 100.00%, while the minimum was 0.00%. Private colleges were much more active than public ones, as the former interviewed 55.11% of departing students vs only 33.08% for public colleges. The median for public colleges was only 10%; for private ones, 65%.

Importance of Exit Interviews on Retention Strategy

How important have exit interviews been in developing and implementing your retention strategy?

On students who did not graduate, 33.33% said exit interviews were useful, and 26.19% said they were somewhat useful. 14.29% gave no answer. 11.90% said they were absolutely invaluable, and 7.14% each said that interviews were not really too useful or were virtually useless.

On graduating students, 26.82% reported exit interviews as having been useful, and 23.82% gave no answer. 23.43% said interviews were somewhat useful, and 9.52% each gave the absolutely invaluable, not really too useful, and virtually useless responses.

Alerts to Pinpoint Students Not Engaged in Extra-Curricular Activities

We asked: Does the college maintain any records that enable it to pinpoint students who are not engaged in any or few extra-curricular activities?

54.76% said no, 40.48% said yes, and 4.76% gave no answer. Private colleges were much more likely than public ones to maintain an alert system – 57.14% did vs. only 23.81% for public colleges. In general, the higher the tuition charged, the greater the likelihood that such a system is in effect.

Role of Information Literacy in Retention

We asked: Your college's information literacy policy is best approximated by which statement:

38.10% said there is no specific information or computer literacy requirement, and 38.10% said the college teaches information/computer literacy within the framework of the basic English Writing Course or other basic course. 9.52% said the college requires one or more three credit information literacy or computer literacy course for graduation. 7.14% claimed the college requires a one or two credit information literacy or computer literacy course for graduation, and 7.14% gave no answer.

In general public colleges were much more likely than private ones to have some form of information and/or computer literacy requirement for graduation.

Percentage of Colleges that Offer Childcare Services

We asked: Does the college offer childcare services for students with children?

76.19% said no, 21.43% said yes, and 2.38% gave no answer. Public colleges were twice as likely as private ones to offer childcare services to students.

Importance to Retention of the College Office of Financial Aid

We asked: On a scale of 1 – 5 with "1" as very important and "5" as unimportant, how critical are the following student services for success in retention.

78.57% said the office of financial aid was very important, and 14.29% stated it was important. 4.76% claimed it was somewhat important, and 2.38% who gave no answer. 0.00% said it was infrequently important or not really important.

Importance to Retention of the Office of Career Services

Offices of career services were important, according to 50.00% of respondents. 19.05% said they were very important, and 16.67% said they were somewhat important. 7.14% said they were infrequently important, 4.76% gave no answer, and 2.38% said they were not really important.

Importance to Retention of the Office of Academic Advising

71.43% said academic advising was very important, 21.43% said it was important, 4.76% said it was somewhat important, 2.38% gave no answer, and 0.00% each said academic advising was not really important or infrequently important.

Importance of Tutoring Services for Student Retention

Learning services/tutoring services were reported to be very important by 64.29%, followed by 21.43% who claimed they are important. 11.90% said they are somewhat important. 2.38% gave no answer, and 0.00% said they were infrequently important or that they were not really important.

Identification of Student Intervention Threshholds

We asked: Does the college identify high risk students and then intervene at certain thresh-holds such as number of classes or assignments missed, or low grade point average?

85.71% said yes, 11.90% said no, and 2.38% gave no answer.

View of Efforts to Help Students at Risk of Dropping Out

We asked: Which phrase best describes your view of your college's efforts to reach out to and help students at high risk for dropping out?

40.48% said we make a fairly considerable effort and do as well as most. 21.43% said we make a great effort but without great results, and 11.90% said we make a great effort and we have very good results. 11.90% said we don't do enough and are not really good at what we do, and 11.90% said we don't do enough, and our present efforts are passable at best. 2.38% gave no answer.

College Spending on Tutoring in the Past Year

We asked: What is the college spending (in US$) on tutoring for all students?

The past-year mean was $78,480.00, the median was $44,000.00, the maximum was $550,000.00, and the minimum was $5,000.00.

Expected College Spending on Tutoring in the Next Year

Next-year expected mean spending was $80,280.00. The expected median was $45,000.00, the expected maximum was $562,000.00, and the expected minimum was $5,000.00. The one year increase for colleges in the sample was modest: about 2.3%.

Evaluation of the Impact of College Tutoring on Retention

We asked: Which phrase best describes your attitude towards the impact that the college tutoring program has had on student retention?

40.48% claimed we need to hire more tutors, train them better, or both. 40.48% said we have a good tutoring program that has helped us to maintain or increase our retention levels. 9.52% gave no answer, while 7.14% said our tutoring program is excellent and is a key factor in our maintenance of a higher than expected retention level. 2.38% reported I don't think that tutoring can have a big impact on retention.

Percentage of Colleges that Maintain Student Advisory Centers in Student Residence Halls

We asked: Does the college have student advisory centers located in residence halls?

83.33% said no, 9.52% gave no answer, and 7.14% said yes.

Percentage of Colleges that have Ever Hired a Consultant to Review or Advise Academic Advising

We asked: To the best of your knowledge, has the college ever hired a consultant to review or advise on the college academic advising services?

64.29% said no, 23.81% said yes, and 11.90% gave no answer.

Budget for the College Department of Academic Advising

We asked: What is the total annual budget (in US$), including spending for salaries, of the college's academic advising unit?

The mean was $577,700.41, the median was $245,000.00, the maximum was $3,000,000.00, and the minimum was $0.00.

Recent Changes in the Level of Financial Aid

We asked: Over the past two years the college's financial aid has:

50.00% said financial aid remained about the same in real terms. 30.95% said it became somewhat more generous, and 7.14% said it became somewhat less generous. 7.14% gave no answer. 4.76% said it became much less generous, and 0.00% said that it became much more generous.

Impact of Tuition Increases on Retention

We asked: My personal feeling about tuition levels and the financial situation of our student body is that:

It has become more and more difficult for our students to pay for college, said 52.38%. 33.33% claimed the overall financial burden on our students has not changed much in recent years. 7.14% said our aid programs and a strong economy have actually reduced the financial burden on our students in recent years, and 7.14% gave no answer.

Changes in the Rate of Student Retention for First Year Students Entering the Second Year

We asked: The college's retention rate for first year students entering the second year has:

52.38% of all participants said it remained the same in the past two years, followed by 23.81% who said it increased, and 16.67% who said that it had decreased. 7.14% gave no answer.

Percentage of Those who Drop Out Who do So Largely for Financial Reasons

We asked: About what percentage of students who drop out do you believe do so primarily for economic reasons?

The mean was 41.53%, the median was 35.00%, the maximum was 90.00%, and the minimum was 10.00%.

Expectations for Retention Rates

We asked: Over the past few years your best honest estimate is that:

Our retention rates will probably stay about the same, reported 54.76%. 33.33% said our retention rates will increase, 7.14% gave no answer, and 4.76% said our retention rates will probably decline. This is despite the fact that the same sample shows a more than 10% decline in retention rates over the past five years, so this optimism should be seen in light of these facts.

Adult Education Program Retention Compared to Traditional College Program Retention

We asked: If your college has any of the following types of programs rank their retention rates relative to your man college program.

On adult education programs, 64.29% gave no answer, and 14.29% said the retention rates would stay about the same. 11.90% said they would be above traditional programs, 7.14% reported that they would be below traditional programs, and 2.38% said they would be much below traditional programs. 0.00% said they would be much above traditional programs.

Distance Education Program Retention Compared to Traditional College Program Retention

On distance education, 52.38% gave no answer, and 30.95% said retention rates would be about the same. 11.90% said they would be below traditional programs, and 2.38% said they would be much below traditional programs. 2.38% said they would be above traditional programs, and 0.00% said they would be much above traditional programs.

Table 1.1 How much did the college spend (in US $) on consulting services to aid in student retention in the past year? (exclude spending on conference which we ask about separately)

	Mean	Median	Minimum	Maximum
Entire sample	5870.97	0.00	0.00	50000.00

Table 1.2 How much did the college spend (in US $) on consulting services to aid in student retention in the past year? (exclude spending on conference which we ask about separately) Broken out for public and private colleges

Your college is:	Mean	Median	Minimum	Maximum
A public college	5666.67	0.00	0.00	50000.00
A private college	6000.00	0.00	0.00	25000.00

Table 1.3 How much did the college spend (in US $) on consulting services to aid in student retention in the past year? (exclude spending on conference which we ask about separately) Broken out by enrollment

Enrollment	Mean	Median	Minimum	Maximum
Less than 1000	1250.00	0.00	0.00	10000.00
1000 - 2999	2111.11	0.00	0.00	14000.00
3000 - 7000	5333.33	0.00	0.00	25000.00
More than 7000	21000.00	20000.00	0.00	50000.00

Table 1.4 How much did the college spend (in US $) on consulting services to aid in student retention in the past year? (exclude spending on conference which we ask about separately) Broken out by college type or Carnegie class

College type or Carnegie class	Mean	Median	Minimum	Maximum
Carnegie Class 4-year or MA degree granting institution, Community College	2807.69	0.00	0.00	25000.00
Carnegie Class Research universities*	21800.00	20000.00	0.00	50000.00

*Includes R1, R2 and Doctoral-Level Institutions

Table 1.5 How much did the college spend (in US $) on consulting services to aid in student retention in the past year? (exclude spending on conference which we ask about separately) Broken out by tuition, $

Tuition, $	Mean	Median	Minimum	Maximum
Less than 10000	2250.00	500.00	0.00	10000.00
10000 - 20999	16666.67	0.00	0.00	50000.00
21000 - 30000	1818.18	0.00	0.00	20000.00
More than 30000	10444.44	10000.00	0.00	25000.00

Table 2.1 How much do you expect that the college will spend (in US $) on consulting services to aid in student retention in the next year? (exclude spending on conference which we ask about separately)

	Mean	Median	Minimum	Maximum
Entire sample	11983.33	0.00	0.00	125000.00

Table 2.2 How much do you expect that the college will spend (in US $) on consulting services to aid in student retention in the next year? (exclude spending on conference which we ask about separately) Broken out for public and private colleges

Your college is:	Mean	Median	Minimum	Maximum
A public college	24450.00	4750.00	0.00	125000.00
A private college	5750.00	0.00	0.00	25000.00

Table 2.3 How much do you expect that the college will spend (in US $) on consulting services to aid in student retention in the next year? (exclude spending on conference which we ask about separately) Broken out by enrollment

Enrollment	Mean	Median	Minimum	Maximum
Less than 1000	1250.00	0.00	0.00	10000.00
1000 - 2999	1666.67	0.00	0.00	14000.00
3000 - 7000	25500.00	7500.00	0.00	125000.00
More than 7000	26250.00	22500.00	10000.00	50000.00

Table 2.4 How much do you expect that the college will spend (in US $) on consulting services to aid in student retention in the next year? (exclude spending on conference which we ask about separately) Broken out by college type or Carnegie class

College type or Carnegie class	Mean	Median	Minimum	Maximum
Carnegie Class 4-year or MA degree granting institution, Community College	9634.62	0.00	0.00	125000.00
Carnegie Class Research universities	27250.00	22500.00	14000.00	50000.00

Table 2.5 How much do you expect that the college will spend (in US $) on consulting services to aid in student retention in the next year? (exclude spending on conference which we ask about separately) Broken out by tuition, $

Tuition, $	Mean	Median	Minimum	Maximum
Less than 10000	20642.86	2000.00	0.00	125000.00
10000 - 20999	33333.33	50000.00	0.00	50000.00
21000 - 30000	1909.09	0.00	0.00	20000.00
More than 30000	10444.44	10000.00	0.00	25000.00

Table 3.1 Does the college have a dean or other high level administrator whose primary responsibility is to maintain or increase student retention?

	No Answer	Yes	No
Entire sample	2.38%	52.38%	45.24%

Table 3.2 Does the college have a dean or other high level administrator whose primary responsibility is to maintain or increase student retention? Broken out for public and private colleges

Your college is:	No Answer	Yes	No
A public college	4.76%	42.86%	52.38%
A private college	0.00%	61.90%	38.10%

Table 3.3 Does the college have a dean or other high level administrator whose primary responsibility is to maintain or increase student retention? Broken out by enrollment

Enrollment	No Answer	Yes	No
Less than 1000	0.00%	50.00%	50.00%
1000 - 2999	0.00%	60.00%	40.00%
3000 - 7000	0.00%	35.71%	64.29%
More than 7000	10.00%	70.00%	20.00%

Table 3.4 Does the college have a dean or other high level administrator whose primary responsibility is to maintain or increase student retention? Broken out by college type or Carnegie class

College type or Carnegie class	No Answer	Yes	No
Carnegie Class 4-year or MA degree granting institution, Community College	0.00%	47.06%	52.94%
Carnegie Class Research universities	12.50%	75.00%	12.50%

Table 3.5 Does the college have a dean or other high level administrator whose primary responsibility is to maintain or increase student retention? Broken out by tuition, $

Tuition, $	No Answer	Yes	No
Less than 10000	8.33%	41.67%	50.00%
10000 - 20999	0.00%	50.00%	50.00%
21000 - 30000	0.00%	46.15%	53.85%
More than 30000	0.00%	72.73%	27.27%

Table 4.1 What was the college's fall to fall retention rate for first year students in the fall 2013 to fall 2014 school year?

These older figures are being provided to serve as a point of comparison with the 2018-19 school year, the data for which is found two pages ahead.

	Mean	Median	Minimum	Maximum
Entire sample	72.33	74.50	20.00	96.00

Table 4.2 What was the college's fall to fall retention rate for first year students in the fall 2013 to fall 2014 school year? Broken out for public and private colleges

Your college is:	Mean	Median	Minimum	Maximum
A public college	71.56	74.00	20.00	92.00
A private college	73.10	76.00	37.00	96.00

Table 4.3 What was the college's fall to fall retention rate for first year students in the fall 2013 to fall 2014 school year? Broken out by enrollment

Enrollment	Mean	Median	Minimum	Maximum
Less than 1000	68.00	70.00	52.00	82.00
1000 - 2999	61.82	68.15	20.00	86.00
3000 - 7000	75.41	76.00	59.00	85.00
More than 7000	84.25	87.75	70.00	96.00

Table 4.4 What was the college's fall to fall retention rate for first year students in the fall 2013 to fall 2014 school year? Broken out by college type or Carnegie class

College type or Carnegie class	Mean	Median	Minimum	Maximum
Carnegie Class 4-year or MA degree granting institution, Community College	70.11	72.00	20.00	89.00
Carnegie Class Research universities	84.15	83.75	72.50	96.00

Table 4.5 What was the college's fall to fall retention rate for first year students in the fall 2013 to fall 2014 school year? Broken out by tuition, $

Tuition, $	Mean	Median	Minimum	Maximum
Less than 10000	64.80	70.00	20.00	92.00
10000 - 20999	80.50	79.00	72.50	89.00
21000 - 30000	71.16	72.00	37.00	85.00
More than 30000	77.29	76.95	52.00	96.00

Table 5.1 What was the college's fall to fall retention rate for part time students from fall 2018 to fall 2019?

	Mean	Median	Minimum	Maximum
Entire sample	68.86	72.00	33.00	89.50

Table 5.2 What was the college's fall to fall retention rate for part time students from fall 2018 to fall 2019? Broken out for public and private colleges

Your college is:	Mean	Median	Minimum	Maximum
A public college	67.64	72.80	40.00	81.50
A private college	69.96	72.00	33.00	89.50

Table 5.3 What was the college's fall to fall retention rate for part time students from fall 2018 to fall 2019? Broken out by enrollment

Enrollment	Mean	Median	Minimum	Maximum
Less than 1000	55.75	59.00	33.00	72.00
1000 - 2999	61.03	59.05	40.00	86.00
3000 - 7000	76.70	78.00	71.00	81.50
More than 7000	80.03	79.50	71.60	89.50

Table 5.4 What was the college's fall to fall retention rate for part time students from fall 2018 to fall 2019? Broken out by college type or Carnegie class

College type or Carnegie class	Mean	Median	Minimum	Maximum
Carnegie Class 4-year or MA degree granting institution, Community College	64.96	71.50	33.00	86.00
Carnegie Class Research universities	78.24	78.00	71.10	89.50

Table 5.5 What was the college's fall to fall retention rate for part time students from fall 2018 to fall 2019? Broken out by tuition, $

Tuition, $	Mean	Median	Minimum	Maximum
Less than 10000	65.17	74.00	40.00	81.50
10000 - 20999	71.30	71.30	71.00	71.60
21000 - 30000	61.50	66.00	33.00	79.00
More than 30000	77.27	79.50	58.00	89.50

Table 6 What was the retention rate for the following specific kinds of students?

Table 6.1.1 What was the retention rate for graduate students?

	Mean	Median	Minimum	Maximum
Entire sample	86.50	90.50	70.00	92.00

Table 6.1.2 What was the retention rate for graduate students? Broken out for public and private colleges

Your college is:	Mean	Median	Minimum	Maximum
A public college	80.50	80.50	70.00	91.00
A private college	89.50	91.00	84.00	92.00

Table 6.1.3 What was the retention rate for graduate students? Broken out by enrollment

Enrollment	Mean	Median	Minimum	Maximum
Less than 1000	88.00	88.00	84.00	92.00
3000 - 7000	80.00	80.00	70.00	90.00
More than 7000	91.50	91.50	91.00	92.00

Table 6.1.4 What was the retention rate for graduate students? Broken out by college type or Carnegie class

College type or Carnegie class	Mean	Median	Minimum	Maximum
Carnegie Class 4-year or MA degree granting institution, Community College	84.00	87.00	70.00	92.00
Carnegie Class Research universities	91.50	91.50	91.00	92.00

Table 6.1.5 What was the retention rate for graduate students? Broken out by tuition, $

Tuition, $	Mean	Median	Minimum	Maximum
Less than 10000	70.00	70.00	70.00	70.00
21000 - 30000	89.00	91.00	84.00	92.00
More than 30000	91.00	91.00	90.00	92.00

Table 6.3.1 What was the retention rate for distance learning/hybrid learning students?

	Mean	Median	Minimum	Maximum
Entire sample	68.00	76.00	30.00	90.00

Table 6.3.2 What was the retention rate for distance learning/hybrid learning students? Broken out for public and private colleges

Your college is:	Mean	Median	Minimum	Maximum
A public college	30.00	30.00	30.00	30.00
A private college	80.67	90.00	62.00	90.00

Table 6.3.3 What was the retention rate for distance learning/hybrid learning students? Broken out by enrollment

Enrollment	Mean	Median	Minimum	Maximum
Less than 1000	76.00	76.00	62.00	90.00
1000 - 2999	30.00	30.00	30.00	30.00
3000 - 7000	90.00	90.00	90.00	90.00

Table 6.3.4 What was the retention rate for distance learning/hybrid learning students? Broken out by college type or Carnegie class

College type or Carnegie class	Mean	Median	Minimum	Maximum
Carnegie Class 4-year or MA degree granting institution, Community College	68.00	76.00	30.00	90.00

Table 6.3.5 What was the retention rate for distance learning/hybrid learning students? Broken out by tuition, $

Tuition, $	Mean	Median	Minimum	Maximum
Less than 10000	30.00	30.00	30.00	30.00
21000 - 30000	76.00	76.00	62.00	90.00
More than 30000	90.00	90.00	90.00	90.00

Table 6.4.1 What was the retention rate for foreign students?

	Mean	Median	Minimum	Maximum
Entire sample	73.89	83.00	30.00	98.00

Table 6.4.2 What was the retention rate for foreign students? Broken out for public and private colleges

Your college is:	Mean	Median	Minimum	Maximum
A public college	71.67	80.00	52.00	83.00
A private college	75.00	87.00	30.00	98.00

Table 6.4.3 What was the retention rate for foreign students? Broken out by enrollment

Enrollment	Mean	Median	Minimum	Maximum
Less than 1000	65.00	70.50	30.00	89.00
1000 - 2999	52.00	52.00	52.00	52.00
3000 - 7000	87.50	87.50	83.00	92.00
More than 7000	89.00	89.00	80.00	98.00

Table 6.4.4 What was the retention rate for foreign students? Broken out by college type or Carnegie class

College type or Carnegie class	Mean	Median	Minimum	Maximum
Carnegie Class 4-year or MA degree granting institution, Community College	70.88	81.50	30.00	92.00
Carnegie Class Research universities	98.00	98.00	98.00	98.00

Table 6.4.5 What was the retention rate for foreign students? Broken out by tuition, $

Tuition, $	Mean	Median	Minimum	Maximum
Less than 10000	81.50	81.50	80.00	83.00
21000 - 30000	55.75	54.00	30.00	85.00
More than 30000	93.00	92.00	89.00	98.00

Table 6.5.1 What was the retention rate for adult students over age 30 (or some reasonable equivalent)?

	Mean	Median	Minimum	Maximum
Entire sample	63.60	61.00	45.00	99.00

Table 6.5.2 What was the retention rate for adult students over age 30 (or some reasonable equivalent)? Broken out for public and private colleges

Your college is:	Mean	Median	Minimum	Maximum
A public college	56.33	61.00	45.00	63.00
A private college	74.50	74.50	50.00	99.00

Table 6.5.3 What was the retention rate for adult students over age 30 (or some reasonable equivalent)? Broken out by enrollment

Enrollment	Mean	Median	Minimum	Maximum
Less than 1000	50.00	50.00	50.00	50.00
1000 - 2999	53.00	53.00	45.00	61.00
3000 - 7000	63.00	63.00	63.00	63.00
More than 7000	99.00	99.00	99.00	99.00

Table 6.5.4 What was the retention rate for adult students over age 30 (or some reasonable equivalent)? Broken out by college type or Carnegie class

College type or Carnegie class	Mean	Median	Minimum	Maximum
Carnegie Class 4-year or MA degree granting institution, Community College	54.75	55.50	45.00	63.00
Carnegie Class Research universities	99.00	99.00	99.00	99.00

Table 6.5.5 What was the retention rate for adult students over age 30 (or some reasonable equivalent)? Broken out by tuition, $

Tuition, $	Mean	Median	Minimum	Maximum
Less than 10000	54.00	54.00	45.00	63.00
21000 - 30000	55.50	55.50	50.00	61.00
More than 30000	99.00	99.00	99.00	99.00

Table 7.1 For the last year for which such data is available, what percentage of students who start at the college as fall term freshmen graduate the college?

	Mean	Median	Minimum	Maximum
Entire sample	55.12	56.00	18.00	87.00

Table 7.2 For the last year for which such data is available, what percentage of students who start at the college as fall term freshmen graduate the college? Broken out for public and private colleges

Your college is:	Mean	Median	Minimum	Maximum
A public college	48.77	49.50	18.00	77.00
A private college	60.46	59.00	37.00	87.00

Table 7.3 For the last year for which such data is available, what percentage of students who start at the college as fall term freshmen graduate the college? Broken out by enrollment

Enrollment	Mean	Median	Minimum	Maximum
Less than 1000	52.57	49.00	37.00	79.00
1000 - 2999	51.85	56.00	18.00	68.00
3000 - 7000	55.56	57.50	34.00	77.30
More than 7000	60.88	60.50	32.00	87.00

Table 7.4 For the last year for which such data is available, what percentage of students who start at the college as fall term freshmen graduate the college? Broken out by college type or Carnegie class

College type or Carnegie class	Mean	Median	Minimum	Maximum
Carnegie Class 4-year or MA degree granting institution, Community College	52.40	53.00	18.00	79.00
Carnegie Class Research universities	68.27	70.00	45.10	87.00

Table 7.5 For the last year for which such data is available, what percentage of students who start at the college as fall term freshmen graduate the college? Broken out by tuition, $

Tuition, $	Mean	Median	Minimum	Maximum
Less than 10000	43.98	42.90	18.00	77.00
10000 - 20999	50.02	56.00	32.00	59.00
21000 - 30000	57.42	58.00	37.00	79.00
More than 30000	63.82	64.71	38.00	87.00

If you have had particular success in increasing retention rates for any specific group defined by any criteria -- race, SAT level, academic major, geographic origin, or any other criteria - explain how you achieved this success. Broken out by college type or Carnegie class

Carnegie Class 4-year or MA degree granting institution, Community College

1) Not success yet but identified male students of color as a group that is in need.
2) 1st generation: we use peer coaches to help with 1st term integration
3) We have focused on financial incentives and academic initiatives that are geared towards classroom teaching and not cohorts of students.
4) Retention for racial and ethnic minorities increased when a particular fraternity known for its hostility to minority groups was removed from campus.
5) We have been improving our retention rates for our general bachelor's degree population as a whole for the last two years. We have streamlined processes, developed various retention campaigns, trained staff with professional development, and looking at barriers to our students' success.
6) New football coach and football academic success camp
7) Have increased retention of Pell-eligible students with a FY-to-Sophy one-time scholarship incentive of $1000. Tried this last year and increased retention in the group 4% so are continuing it this year.
8) The majority of our gains in retention over the last few years were due to investment in our FYE program.
9) We recently hired a Sophomore year counselor to increase the retention rate from a student's sophomore to junior years.
10) N/A
11) None specifically
12) Students with disabilities retain Fall to Fall at a rate of 85%.
13) do not know

Carnegie Class Research Universities

1) Our summer bridge program for low-income, first generation students has had a huge success rate for many years.
2) First year success seminar Mentoring Summer Bridge Program
3) N/A
4) Unsure

Table 8 Using a scale of 1-4, rank the impact on retention of the following on student retention:

Table 8.1.1 Using a scale of 1-4, rank the impact on retention of terms of student financial assistance

	No Answer	Does not have much of an impact	Has some impact	Has a significant impact	Has a dramatic impact
Entire sample	0.00%	0.00%	23.81%	33.33%	42.86%

Table 8.1.2 Using a scale of 1-4, rank the impact on retention of terms of student financial assistance Broken out for public and private colleges

Your college is:	No Answer	Does not have much of an impact	Has some impact	Has a significant impact	Has a dramatic impact
A public college	0.00%	0.00%	23.81%	38.10%	38.10%
A private college	0.00%	0.00%	23.81%	28.57%	47.62%

Table 8.1.3 Using a scale of 1-4, rank the impact on retention of terms of student financial assistance Broken out by enrollment

Enrollment	No Answer	Does not have much of an impact	Has some impact	Has a significant impact	Has a dramatic impact
Less than 1000	0.00%	0.00%	0.00%	25.00%	75.00%
1000 - 2999	0.00%	0.00%	30.00%	20.00%	50.00%
3000 - 7000	0.00%	0.00%	28.57%	42.86%	28.57%
More than 7000	0.00%	0.00%	30.00%	40.00%	30.00%

Table 8.1.4 Using a scale of 1-4, rank the impact on retention of terms of student financial assistance Broken out by college type or Carnegie class

College type or Carnegie class	No Answer	Does not have much of an impact	Has some impact	Has a significant impact	Has a dramatic impact
Carnegie Class 4-year or MA degree granting institution, Community College	0.00%	0.00%	20.59%	38.24%	41.18%
Carnegie Class Research universities	0.00%	0.00%	37.50%	12.50%	50.00%

Table 8.1.5 Using a scale of 1-4, rank the impact on retention of terms of student financial assistance Broken out by tuition, $

Tuition, $	No Answer	Does not have much of an impact	Has some impact	Has a significant impact	Has a dramatic impact
Less than 10000	0.00%	0.00%	25.00%	33.33%	41.67%
10000 - 20999	0.00%	0.00%	16.67%	33.33%	50.00%
21000 - 30000	0.00%	0.00%	23.08%	38.46%	38.46%
More than 30000	0.00%	0.00%	27.27%	27.27%	45.45%

Table 8.2.1 Using a scale of 1-4, rank the impact on retention of severity in grading

	No Answer	Does not have much of an impact	Has some impact	Has a significant impact	Has a dramatic impact
Entire sample	2.38%	19.05%	50.00%	26.19%	2.38%

Table 8.2.2 Using a scale of 1-4, rank the impact on retention of severity in grading Broken out for public and private colleges

Your college is:	No Answer	Does not have much of an impact	Has some impact	Has a significant impact	Has a dramatic impact
A public college	0.00%	9.52%	71.43%	19.05%	0.00%
A private college	4.76%	28.57%	28.57%	33.33%	4.76%

Table 8.2.3 Using a scale of 1-4, rank the impact on retention of severity in grading Broken out by enrollment

Enrollment	No Answer	Does not have much of an impact	Has some impact	Has a significant impact	Has a dramatic impact
Less than 1000	12.50%	37.50%	25.00%	12.50%	12.50%
1000 - 2999	0.00%	20.00%	30.00%	50.00%	0.00%
3000 - 7000	0.00%	0.00%	78.57%	21.43%	0.00%
More than 7000	0.00%	30.00%	50.00%	20.00%	0.00%

Table 8.2.4 Using a scale of 1-4, rank the impact on retention of severity in grading Broken out by college type or Carnegie class

College type or Carnegie class	No Answer	Does not have much of an impact	Has some impact	Has a significant impact	Has a dramatic impact
Carnegie Class 4-year or MA degree granting institution, Community College	2.94%	14.71%	55.88%	23.53%	2.94%
Carnegie Class Research universities	0.00%	37.50%	25.00%	37.50%	0.00%

Table 8.2.5 Using a scale of 1-4, rank the impact on retention of severity in grading Broken out by tuition, $

Tuition, $	No Answer	Does not have much of an impact	Has some impact	Has a significant impact	Has a dramatic impact
Less than 10000	0.00%	8.33%	83.33%	8.33%	0.00%
10000 - 20999	0.00%	16.67%	83.33%	0.00%	0.00%
21000 - 30000	7.69%	23.08%	15.38%	53.85%	0.00%
More than 30000	0.00%	27.27%	36.36%	27.27%	9.09%

Table 8.3.1 Using a scale of 1-4, rank the impact on retention of access to tutoring services

	No Answer	Does not have much of an impact	Has some impact	Has a significant impact	Has a dramatic impact
Entire sample	2.38%	7.14%	33.33%	57.14%	0.00%

Table 8.3.2 Using a scale of 1-4, rank the impact on retention of access to tutoring services Broken out for public and private colleges

Your college is:	No Answer	Does not have much of an impact	Has some impact	Has a significant impact	Has a dramatic impact
A public college	4.76%	14.29%	33.33%	47.62%	0.00%
A private college	0.00%	0.00%	33.33%	66.67%	0.00%

Table 8.3.3 Using a scale of 1-4, rank the impact on retention of access to tutoring services Broken out by enrollment

Enrollment	No Answer	Does not have much of an impact	Has some impact	Has a significant impact	Has a dramatic impact
Less than 1000	0.00%	0.00%	25.00%	75.00%	0.00%
1000 - 2999	0.00%	0.00%	50.00%	50.00%	0.00%
3000 - 7000	0.00%	7.14%	35.71%	57.14%	0.00%
More than 7000	10.00%	20.00%	20.00%	50.00%	0.00%

Table 8.3.4 Using a scale of 1-4, rank the impact on retention of access to tutoring services Broken out by college type or Carnegie class

College type or Carnegie class	No Answer	Does not have much of an impact	Has some impact	Has a significant impact	Has a dramatic impact
Carnegie Class 4-year or MA degree granting institution, Community College	0.00%	2.94%	38.24%	58.82%	0.00%
Carnegie Class Research universities	12.50%	25.00%	12.50%	50.00%	0.00%

Table 8.3.5 Using a scale of 1-4, rank the impact on retention of access to tutoring services Broken out by tuition, $

Tuition, $	No Answer	Does not have much of an impact	Has some impact	Has a significant impact	Has a dramatic impact
Less than 10000	0.00%	16.67%	25.00%	58.33%	0.00%
10000 - 20999	0.00%	16.67%	33.33%	50.00%	0.00%
21000 - 30000	7.69%	0.00%	46.15%	46.15%	0.00%
More than 30000	0.00%	0.00%	27.27%	72.73%	0.00%

Table 8.4.1 Using a scale of 1-4, rank the impact on retention of changes in the academic reputation of the college

	No Answer	Does not have much of an impact	Has some impact	Has a significant impact	Has a dramatic impact
Entire sample	2.38%	38.10%	42.86%	11.90%	4.76%

Table 8.4.2 Using a scale of 1-4, rank the impact on retention of changes in the academic reputation of the college Broken out for public and private colleges

Your college is:	No Answer	Does not have much of an impact	Has some impact	Has a significant impact	Has a dramatic impact
A public college	0.00%	47.62%	47.62%	4.76%	0.00%
A private college	4.76%	28.57%	38.10%	19.05%	9.52%

Table 8.4.3 Using a scale of 1-4, rank the impact on retention of changes in the academic reputation of the college Broken out by enrollment

Enrollment	No Answer	Does not have much of an impact	Has some impact	Has a significant impact	Has a dramatic impact
Less than 1000	12.50%	12.50%	50.00%	12.50%	12.50%
1000 - 2999	0.00%	40.00%	40.00%	10.00%	10.00%
3000 - 7000	0.00%	42.86%	50.00%	7.14%	0.00%
More than 7000	0.00%	50.00%	30.00%	20.00%	0.00%

Table 8.4.4 Using a scale of 1-4, rank the impact on retention of changes in the academic reputation of the college Broken out by college type or Carnegie class

College type or Carnegie class	No Answer	Does not have much of an impact	Has some impact	Has a significant impact	Has a dramatic impact
Carnegie Class 4-year or MA degree granting institution, Community College	2.94%	35.29%	47.06%	8.82%	5.88%
Carnegie Class Research universities	0.00%	50.00%	25.00%	25.00%	0.00%

Table 8.4.5 Using a scale of 1-4, rank the impact on retention of changes in the academic reputation of the college Broken out by tuition, $

Tuition, $	No Answer	Does not have much of an impact	Has some impact	Has a significant impact	Has a dramatic impact
Less than 10000	0.00%	58.33%	41.67%	0.00%	0.00%
10000 - 20999	0.00%	33.33%	50.00%	16.67%	0.00%
21000 - 30000	7.69%	15.38%	53.85%	15.38%	7.69%
More than 30000	0.00%	45.45%	27.27%	18.18%	9.09%

Table 8.5.1 Using a scale of 1-4, rank the impact on retention of access to academic and/or psychological counseling services

	No Answer	Does not have much of an impact	Has some impact	Has a significant impact	Has a dramatic impact
Entire sample	0.00%	4.76%	26.19%	57.14%	11.90%

Table 8.5.2 Using a scale of 1-4, rank the impact on retention of access to academic and/or psychological counseling services Broken out for public and private colleges

Your college is:	No Answer	Does not have much of an impact	Has some impact	Has a significant impact	Has a dramatic impact
A public college	0.00%	4.76%	23.81%	57.14%	14.29%
A private college	0.00%	4.76%	28.57%	57.14%	9.52%

Table 8.5.3 Using a scale of 1-4, rank the impact on retention of access to academic and/or psychological counseling services Broken out by enrollment

Enrollment	No Answer	Does not have much of an impact	Has some impact	Has a significant impact	Has a dramatic impact
Less than 1000	0.00%	12.50%	37.50%	50.00%	0.00%
1000 - 2999	0.00%	0.00%	30.00%	60.00%	10.00%
3000 - 7000	0.00%	0.00%	28.57%	50.00%	21.43%
More than 7000	0.00%	10.00%	10.00%	70.00%	10.00%

Table 8.5.4 Using a scale of 1-4, rank the impact on retention of access to academic and/or psychological counseling services Broken out by college type or Carnegie class

College type or Carnegie class	No Answer	Does not have much of an impact	Has some impact	Has a significant impact	Has a dramatic impact
Carnegie Class 4-year or MA degree granting institution, Community College	0.00%	2.94%	32.35%	55.88%	8.82%
Carnegie Class Research universities	0.00%	12.50%	0.00%	62.50%	25.00%

Table 8.5.5 Using a scale of 1-4, rank the impact on retention of access to academic and/or psychological counseling services Broken out by tuition, $

Tuition, $	No Answer	Does not have much of an impact	Has some impact	Has a significant impact	Has a dramatic impact
Less than 10000	0.00%	0.00%	8.33%	75.00%	16.67%
10000 - 20999	0.00%	16.67%	33.33%	33.33%	16.67%
21000 - 30000	0.00%	7.69%	38.46%	53.85%	0.00%
More than 30000	0.00%	0.00%	27.27%	54.55%	18.18%

Table 8.6.1 Using a scale of 1-4, rank the impact on retention of general economic conditions

	No Answer	Does not have much of an impact	Has some impact	Has a significant impact	Has a dramatic impact
Entire sample	0.00%	0.00%	38.10%	35.71%	26.19%

Table 8.6.2 Using a scale of 1-4, rank the impact on retention of general economic conditions Broken out for public and private colleges

Your college is:	No Answer	Does not have much of an impact	Has some impact	Has a significant impact	Has a dramatic impact
A public college	0.00%	0.00%	23.81%	38.10%	38.10%
A private college	0.00%	0.00%	52.38%	33.33%	14.29%

Table 8.6.3 Using a scale of 1-4, rank the impact on retention of general economic conditions Broken out by enrollment

Enrollment	No Answer	Does not have much of an impact	Has some impact	Has a significant impact	Has a dramatic impact
Less than 1000	0.00%	0.00%	62.50%	25.00%	12.50%
1000 - 2999	0.00%	0.00%	40.00%	20.00%	40.00%
3000 - 7000	0.00%	0.00%	21.43%	50.00%	28.57%
More than 7000	0.00%	0.00%	40.00%	40.00%	20.00%

Table 8.6.4 Using a scale of 1-4, rank the impact on retention of general economic conditions Broken out by college type or Carnegie class

College type or Carnegie class	No Answer	Does not have much of an impact	Has some impact	Has a significant impact	Has a dramatic impact
Carnegie Class 4-year or MA degree granting institution, Community College	0.00%	0.00%	35.29%	41.18%	23.53%
Carnegie Class Research universities	0.00%	0.00%	50.00%	12.50%	37.50%

Table 8.6.5 Using a scale of 1-4, rank the impact on retention of general economic conditions Broken out by tuition, $

Tuition, $	No Answer	Does not have much of an impact	Has some impact	Has a significant impact	Has a dramatic impact
Less than 10000	0.00%	0.00%	25.00%	33.33%	41.67%
10000 - 20999	0.00%	0.00%	0.00%	50.00%	50.00%
21000 - 30000	0.00%	0.00%	53.85%	30.77%	15.38%
More than 30000	0.00%	0.00%	54.55%	36.36%	9.09%

Table 8.7.1 Using a scale of 1-4, rank the impact on retention of involvement in extra curricular activities

	No Answer	Does not have much of an impact	Has some impact	Has a significant impact	Has a dramatic impact
Entire sample	0.00%	4.76%	30.95%	52.38%	11.90%

Table 8.7.2 Using a scale of 1-4, rank the impact on retention of involvement in extra curricular activities Broken out for public and private colleges

Your college is:	No Answer	Does not have much of an impact	Has some impact	Has a significant impact	Has a dramatic impact
A public college	0.00%	9.52%	38.10%	42.86%	9.52%
A private college	0.00%	0.00%	23.81%	61.90%	14.29%

Table 8.7.3 Using a scale of 1-4, rank the impact on retention of involvement in extra curricular activities Broken out by enrollment

Enrollment	No Answer	Does not have much of an impact	Has some impact	Has a significant impact	Has a dramatic impact
Less than 1000	0.00%	0.00%	0.00%	87.50%	12.50%
1000 - 2999	0.00%	0.00%	30.00%	60.00%	10.00%
3000 - 7000	0.00%	7.14%	50.00%	28.57%	14.29%
More than 7000	0.00%	10.00%	30.00%	50.00%	10.00%

Table 8.7.4 Using a scale of 1-4, rank the impact on retention of involvement in extra curricular activities Broken out by college type or Carnegie class

College type or Carnegie class	No Answer	Does not have much of an impact	Has some impact	Has a significant impact	Has a dramatic impact
Carnegie Class 4-year or MA degree granting institution, Community College	0.00%	2.94%	32.35%	52.94%	11.76%
Carnegie Class Research universities	0.00%	12.50%	25.00%	50.00%	12.50%

Table 8.7.5 Using a scale of 1-4, rank the impact on retention of involvement in extra curricular activities Broken out by tuition, $

Tuition, $	No Answer	Does not have much of an impact	Has some impact	Has a significant impact	Has a dramatic impact
Less than 10000	0.00%	8.33%	33.33%	58.33%	0.00%
10000 - 20999	0.00%	16.67%	33.33%	33.33%	16.67%
21000 - 30000	0.00%	0.00%	23.08%	53.85%	23.08%
More than 30000	0.00%	0.00%	36.36%	54.55%	9.09%

Table 8.8.1 Using a scale of 1-4, rank the impact on retention of quality of residence halls and food service

	No Answer	Does not have much of an impact	Has some impact	Has a significant impact	Has a dramatic impact
Entire sample	0.00%	7.14%	47.62%	30.95%	14.29%

Table 8.8.2 Using a scale of 1-4, rank the impact on retention of quality of residence halls and food service Broken out for public and private colleges

Your college is:	No Answer	Does not have much of an impact	Has some impact	Has a significant impact	Has a dramatic impact
A public college	0.00%	9.52%	52.38%	33.33%	4.76%
A private college	0.00%	4.76%	42.86%	28.57%	23.81%

Table 8.8.3 Using a scale of 1-4, rank the impact on retention of quality of residence halls and food service Broken out by enrollment

Enrollment	No Answer	Does not have much of an impact	Has some impact	Has a significant impact	Has a dramatic impact
Less than 1000	0.00%	0.00%	37.50%	25.00%	37.50%
1000 - 2999	0.00%	10.00%	40.00%	30.00%	20.00%
3000 - 7000	0.00%	7.14%	57.14%	28.57%	7.14%
More than 7000	0.00%	10.00%	50.00%	40.00%	0.00%

Table 8.8.4 Using a scale of 1-4, rank the impact on retention of quality of residence halls and food service Broken out by college type or Carnegie class

College type or Carnegie class	No Answer	Does not have much of an impact	Has some impact	Has a significant impact	Has a dramatic impact
Carnegie Class 4-year or MA degree granting institution, Community College	0.00%	5.88%	47.06%	29.41%	17.65%
Carnegie Class Research universities	0.00%	12.50%	50.00%	37.50%	0.00%

Table 8.8.5 Using a scale of 1-4, rank the impact on retention of quality of residence halls and food service Broken out by tuition, $

Tuition, $	No Answer	Does not have much of an impact	Has some impact	Has a significant impact	Has a dramatic impact
Less than 10000	0.00%	8.33%	41.67%	50.00%	0.00%
10000 - 20999	0.00%	16.67%	33.33%	33.33%	16.67%
21000 - 30000	0.00%	0.00%	53.85%	23.08%	23.08%
More than 30000	0.00%	9.09%	54.55%	18.18%	18.18%

Table 9.1 Approximately what percentage of students who decide to transfer out of or drop out of the college prior to graduation are interviewed by college management to find out their feelings about their experience at the college?

	Mean	Median	Minimum	Maximum
Entire sample	46.16	50.00	0.00	100.00

Table 9.2 Approximately what percentage of students who decide to transfer out of or drop out of the college prior to graduation are interviewed by college management to find out their feelings about their experience at the college? Broken out for public and private colleges

Your college is:	Mean	Median	Minimum	Maximum
A public college	33.08	10.00	0.00	100.00
A private college	55.11	65.00	1.00	100.00

Table 9.3 Approximately what percentage of students who decide to transfer out of or drop out of the college prior to graduation are interviewed by college management to find out their feelings about their experience at the college? Broken out by enrollment

Enrollment	Mean	Median	Minimum	Maximum
Less than 1000	51.71	50.00	1.00	100.00
1000 - 2999	57.50	67.50	0.00	100.00
3000 - 7000	42.00	42.50	0.00	100.00
More than 7000	24.00	10.00	0.00	100.00

Table 9.4 Approximately what percentage of students who decide to transfer out of or drop out of the college prior to graduation are interviewed by college management to find out their feelings about their experience at the college? Broken out by college type or Carnegie class

College type or Carnegie class	Mean	Median	Minimum	Maximum
Carnegie Class 4-year or MA degree granting institution, Community College	47.67	50.00	0.00	100.00
Carnegie Class Research universities	38.00	10.00	0.00	100.00

Table 9.5 Approximately what percentage of students who decide to transfer out of or drop out of the college prior to graduation are interviewed by college management to find out their feelings about their experience at the college? Broken out by tuition, $

Tuition, $	Mean	Median	Minimum	Maximum
Less than 10000	31.25	7.50	0.00	100.00
10000 - 20999	0.00	0.00	0.00	0.00
21000 - 30000	52.50	55.00	1.00	100.00
More than 30000	59.70	71.00	10.00	100.00

Table 10 How important have exit interviews been in developing and implementing your retention strategy?

Table 10.1.1 How important have exit interviews been in developing and implementing retention strategy?

	No Answer	Absolutely Invaluable	Useful	Somewhat Useful	Not really too Useful	Virtually Useless
Entire sample	14.29%	11.90%	33.33%	26.19%	7.14%	7.14%

Table 10.1.2 How important have exit interviews been in developing and implementing retention strategy? Broken out for public and private colleges

Your college is:	No Answer	Absolutely Invaluable	Useful	Somewhat Useful	Not really too Useful	Virtually Useless
A public college	28.57%	14.29%	19.05%	14.29%	14.29%	9.52%
A private college	0.00%	9.52%	47.62%	38.10%	0.00%	4.76%

Table 10.1.3 How important have exit interviews been in developing and implementing retention strategy? Broken out by enrollment

Enrollment	No Answer	Absolutely Invaluable	Useful	Somewhat Useful	Not really too Useful	Virtually Useless
Less than 1000	0.00%	12.50%	50.00%	25.00%	0.00%	12.50%
1000 - 2999	10.00%	20.00%	40.00%	30.00%	0.00%	0.00%
3000 - 7000	14.29%	0.00%	42.86%	14.29%	21.43%	7.14%
More than 7000	30.00%	20.00%	0.00%	40.00%	0.00%	10.00%

Table 10.1.4 How important have exit interviews been in developing and implementing retention strategy? Broken out by college type or Carnegie class

College type or Carnegie class	No Answer	Absolutely Invaluable	Useful	Somewhat Useful	Not really too Useful	Virtually Useless
Carnegie Class 4-year or MA degree granting institution, Community College	8.82%	11.76%	38.24%	23.53%	8.82%	8.82%
Carnegie Class Research universities	37.50%	12.50%	12.50%	37.50%	0.00%	0.00%

Table 10.1.5 How important have exit interviews been in developing and implementing retention strategy? Broken out by tuition, $

Tuition, $	No Answer	Absolutely Invaluable	Useful	Somewhat Useful	Not really too Useful	Virtually Useless
Less than 10000	41.67%	8.33%	16.67%	16.67%	16.67%	0.00%
10000 - 20999	16.67%	16.67%	16.67%	0.00%	16.67%	33.33%
21000 - 30000	0.00%	23.08%	53.85%	15.38%	0.00%	7.69%
More than 30000	0.00%	0.00%	36.36%	63.64%	0.00%	0.00%

Table 10.2.1 How important have exit interviews been in developing and implementing retention strategy for graduating students?

	No Answer	Absolutely Invaluable	Useful	Somewhat Useful	Not really too Useful	Virtually Useless
Entire sample	23.81%	9.52%	26.19%	21.43%	9.52%	9.52%

Table 10.2.2 How important have exit interviews been in developing and implementing retention strategy for graduating students? Broken out for public and private colleges

Your college is:	No Answer	Absolutely Invaluable	Useful	Somewhat Useful	Not really too Useful	Virtually Useless
A public college	28.57%	14.29%	14.29%	14.29%	14.29%	14.29%
A private college	19.05%	4.76%	38.10%	28.57%	4.76%	4.76%

Table 10.2.3 How important have exit interviews been in developing and implementing retention strategy for graduating students? Broken out by enrollment

Enrollment	No Answer	Absolutely Invaluable	Useful	Somewhat Useful	Not really too Useful	Virtually Useless
Less than 1000	12.50%	12.50%	50.00%	25.00%	0.00%	0.00%
1000 - 2999	40.00%	10.00%	30.00%	10.00%	10.00%	0.00%
3000 - 7000	14.29%	0.00%	21.43%	35.71%	21.43%	7.14%
More than 7000	30.00%	20.00%	10.00%	10.00%	0.00%	30.00%

Table 10.2.4 How important have exit interviews been in developing and implementing retention strategy for graduating students? Broken out by college type or Carnegie class

College type or Carnegie class	No Answer	Absolutely Invaluable	Useful	Somewhat Useful	Not really too Useful	Virtually Useless
Carnegie Class 4-year or MA degree granting institution, Community College	20.59%	8.82%	29.41%	20.59%	11.76%	8.82%
Carnegie Class Research universities	37.50%	12.50%	12.50%	25.00%	0.00%	12.50%

Table 10.2.5 How important have exit interviews been in developing and implementing retention strategy for graduating students? Broken out by tuition, $

Tuition, $	No Answer	Absolutely Invaluable	Useful	Somewhat Useful	Not really too Useful	Virtually Useless
Less than 10000	33.33%	8.33%	25.00%	8.33%	16.67%	8.33%
10000 - 20999	16.67%	16.67%	0.00%	16.67%	16.67%	33.33%
21000 - 30000	30.77%	15.38%	30.77%	23.08%	0.00%	0.00%
More than 30000	9.09%	0.00%	36.36%	36.36%	9.09%	9.09%

Table 11.1 Does the college maintain any records that enable it to pinpoint students who are not engaged in any or very few extra-curricular activities?

	No Answer	Yes	No
Entire sample	4.76%	40.48%	54.76%

Table 11.2 Does the college maintain any records that enable it to pinpoint students who are not engaged in any or very few extra-curricular activities? Broken out for public and private colleges

Your college is:	No Answer	Yes	No
A public college	4.76%	23.81%	71.43%
A private college	4.76%	57.14%	38.10%

Table 11.3 Does the college maintain any records that enable it to pinpoint students who are not engaged in any or very few extra-curricular activities? Broken out by enrollment

Enrollment	No Answer	Yes	No
Less than 1000	0.00%	62.50%	37.50%
1000 - 2999	0.00%	30.00%	70.00%
3000 - 7000	0.00%	28.57%	71.43%
More than 7000	20.00%	50.00%	30.00%

Table 11.4 Does the college maintain any records that enable it to pinpoint students who are not engaged in any or very few extra-curricular activities? Broken out by college type or Carnegie class

College type or Carnegie class	No Answer	Yes	No
Carnegie Class 4-year or MA degree granting institution, Community College	0.00%	41.18%	58.82%
Carnegie Class Research universities	25.00%	37.50%	37.50%

Table 11.5 Does the college maintain any records that enable it to pinpoint students who are not engaged in any or very few extra-curricular activities? Broken out by tuition, $

Tuition, $	No Answer	Yes	No
Less than 10000	8.33%	25.00%	66.67%
10000 - 20999	0.00%	33.33%	66.67%
21000 - 30000	0.00%	38.46%	61.54%
More than 30000	9.09%	63.64%	27.27%

Table 12.1 Your college's information literacy policy is best approximated by which statement?

	No Answer	No specific information or computer literacy requirement	Teaches information/computer literacy within the framework of the basic English Writing Course or other basic course	Requires a one or two credit information literacy or computer literacy course for graduation.	Requires one or more three credit information literacy or computer literacy course for graduation.
Entire sample	7.14%	38.10%	38.10%	7.14%	9.52%

Table 12.2 Your college's information literacy policy is best approximated by which statement? Broken out for public and private colleges

Your college is:	No Answer	No specific information or computer literacy requirement	Teaches information/computer literacy within the framework of the basic English Writing Course or other basic course	Requires a one or two credit information literacy or computer literacy course for graduation.	Requires one or more three credit information literacy or computer literacy course for graduation.
A public college	9.52%	33.33%	33.33%	9.52%	14.29%
A private college	4.76%	42.86%	42.86%	4.76%	4.76%

Table 12.3 Your college's information literacy policy is best approximated by which statement? Broken out by enrollment

Enrollment	No Answer	No specific information or computer literacy requirement	Teaches information/computer literacy within the framework of the basic English Writing Course or other basic course	Requires a one or two credit information literacy or computer literacy course for graduation.	Requires one or more three credit information literacy or computer literacy course for graduation.
Less than 1000	0.00%	37.50%	50.00%	12.50%	0.00%
1000 - 2999	0.00%	30.00%	40.00%	0.00%	30.00%
3000 - 7000	0.00%	35.71%	50.00%	7.14%	7.14%
More than 7000	30.00%	50.00%	10.00%	10.00%	0.00%

Table 12.4 Your college's information literacy policy is best approximated by which statement? Broken out by college type or Carnegie class

College type or Carnegie class	No Answer	No specific information or computer literacy requirement	Teaches information/computer literacy within the framework of the basic English Writing Course or other basic course	Requires a one or two credit information literacy or computer literacy course for graduation.	Requires one or more three credit information literacy or computer literacy course for graduation.
Carnegie Class 4-year or MA degree granting institution, Community College	0.00%	38.24%	47.06%	5.88%	8.82%
Carnegie Class Research universities	37.50%	37.50%	0.00%	12.50%	12.50%

Table 12.5 Your college's information literacy policy is best approximated by which statement? Broken out by tuition, $

Tuition, $	No Answer	No specific information or computer literacy requirement	Teaches information/computer literacy within the framework of the basic English Writing Course or other basic course	Requires a one or two credit information literacy or computer literacy course for graduation.	Requires one or more three credit information literacy or computer literacy course for graduation.
Less than 10000	16.67%	8.33%	50.00%	0.00%	25.00%
10000 - 20999	0.00%	83.33%	16.67%	0.00%	0.00%
21000 - 30000	0.00%	46.15%	38.46%	15.38%	0.00%
More than 30000	9.09%	36.36%	36.36%	9.09%	9.09%

Table 13.1 Does the college offer childcare services for students with children?

	No Answer	Yes	No
Entire sample	2.38%	21.43%	76.19%

Table 13.2 Does the college offer childcare services for students with children? Broken out for public and private colleges

Your college is:	No Answer	Yes	No
A public college	0.00%	28.57%	71.43%
A private college	4.76%	14.29%	80.95%

Table 13.3 Does the college offer childcare services for students with children? Broken out by enrollment

Enrollment	No Answer	Yes	No
Less than 1000	0.00%	12.50%	87.50%
1000 - 2999	10.00%	0.00%	90.00%
3000 - 7000	0.00%	35.71%	64.29%
More than 7000	0.00%	30.00%	70.00%

Table 13.4 Does the college offer childcare services for students with children? Broken out by college type or Carnegie class

College type or Carnegie class	No Answer	Yes	No
Carnegie Class 4-year or MA degree granting institution, Community College	2.94%	20.59%	76.47%
Carnegie Class Research universities	0.00%	25.00%	75.00%

Table 13.5 Does the college offer childcare services for students with children? Broken out by tuition, $

Tuition, $	No Answer	Yes	No
Less than 10000	0.00%	33.33%	66.67%
10000 - 20999	0.00%	16.67%	83.33%
21000 - 30000	0.00%	15.38%	84.62%
More than 30000	9.09%	18.18%	72.73%

How important do you consider part time employment for students and the provision of quality internships to be as factors in student retention and have you made efforts to evaluate or improve these services at your college? Broken out by college type or Carnegie class

Carnegie Class 4-year or MA degree granting institution, Community College

1) We have not looked at the retention based on internships or part-time employment. We are currently going through the process of identifying the issues with our retention through an academy with HLC.
2) Strong factor.
3) very important because our degrees are work force related
4) extremely important. We evaluate this through campus surveys and have worked to improve our on-campus employment opportunities.
5) Very important. Federal work-study students are retained at a rate that is 20% or more above non-Federal work-study students.
6) Employment opportunities are important, particularly on-campus, as a large percentage of our students need to work at least part time. Internships have always been high-quality and are coordinated by faculty--these are important for students as they approach graduation. Neither of these areas has been a big emphasis for us in terms of improving retention.
7) This is an important factor that we are trying to improve. Our "work study" program has recently been revamped and moving to an "earn to learn" mentality where students are hired for meaningful educational and professional preparation positions while also being paid.
8) Highly
9) Moderately important. Nearly every degree program offers internship/practicum in its composition, most require them.
10) Have worked past 2 years on improving student experience with work on campus, including FWS, but mixed results. Encourage students to gain internships as prep for jobs but have not achieved 100% participation.
11) Significant - shows connection to learning.
12) We would consider part-time employment to be very important. We've never investigated the impact internships have on retention so I couldn't say for that piece.
13) It is important, but we have not pursued improving this as a retention strategy.

14) In a survey distributed to upper class-man it was indicated that we need to provide more internships.
15) This is important in relationship to financial aid and student engagement.
16) Somewhat important (as a university)
17) Very important and key to our mission
18) Very important
19) Fairly important
20) Part-time employment is a huge factor in retention, as many students feel it necessary to prioritize employment above coursework and class. We are currently strategizing how meet these student needs within the constraints on our campus.
21) Important
22) Very important.
23) Yes, efforts have been made to increase the quality and quantity of internship experiences.
24) ?
25) Extremely important but no efforts to evaluate or improve these services are in place as yet.
26) Very. Yes.
27) No
28) Internships are important, and we have been building support for these in student affairs and academic affairs.

Carnegie Class Research Universities

1) Very important and yes.
2) We think that they are important and there have been some strategies to increase awareness of internships. Advisers are better educated on the importance of this work as well and encourage students to take advantage.
3) Very important. Yet, we are not doing a great job in identifying part-time work for students on campus. We are evaluating this process but do not have an effective plan in place yet.
4) very
5) This is very important. We have made efforts to improve opportunities for students both on and off campus.
6) do not know
7) Strong

Table 14 On a scale of 1-5 with "1" as very important and "5" as unimportant, how critical are the following student services for success in retention.

Table 14.1.1 On a scale of 1-5 with "1" as very important and "5" as unimportant, please specify how critical is the office of financial aid?

	No Answer	Very Important	Important	Somewhat Important	Infrequently Important	Not Really Important
Entire sample	2.38%	78.57%	14.29%	4.76%	0.00%	0.00%

Table 14.1.2 On a scale of 1-5 with "1" as very important and "5" as unimportant, please specify how critical is the office of financial aid? Broken out for public and private colleges

Your college is:	No Answer	Very Important	Important	Somewhat Important	Infrequently Important	Not Really Important
A public college	0.00%	85.71%	9.52%	4.76%	0.00%	0.00%
A private college	4.76%	71.43%	19.05%	4.76%	0.00%	0.00%

Table 14.1.3 On a scale of 1-5 with "1" as very important and "5" as unimportant, please specify how critical is the office of financial aid? Broken out by enrollment

Enrollment	No Answer	Very Important	Important	Somewhat Important	Infrequently Important	Not Really Important
Less than 1000	0.00%	87.50%	0.00%	12.50%	0.00%	0.00%
1000 - 2999	10.00%	70.00%	20.00%	0.00%	0.00%	0.00%
3000 - 7000	0.00%	85.71%	7.14%	7.14%	0.00%	0.00%
More than 7000	0.00%	70.00%	30.00%	0.00%	0.00%	0.00%

Table 14.1.4 On a scale of 1-5 with "1" as very important and "5" as unimportant, please specify how critical is the office of financial aid? Broken out by college type or Carnegie class

College type or Carnegie class	No Answer	Very Important	Important	Somewhat Important	Infrequently Important	Not Really Important
Carnegie Class 4-year or MA degree granting institution, Community College	2.94%	79.41%	11.76%	5.88%	0.00%	0.00%
Carnegie Class Research universities	0.00%	75.00%	25.00%	0.00%	0.00%	0.00%

Table 14.1.5 On a scale of 1-5 with "1" as very important and "5" as unimportant, please specify how critical is the office of financial aid? Broken out by tuition, $

Tuition, $	No Answer	Very Important	Important	Somewhat Important	Infrequently Important	Not Really Important
Less than 10000	0.00%	83.33%	8.33%	8.33%	0.00%	0.00%
10000 - 20999	0.00%	83.33%	16.67%	0.00%	0.00%	0.00%
21000 - 30000	0.00%	84.62%	7.69%	7.69%	0.00%	0.00%
More than 30000	9.09%	63.64%	27.27%	0.00%	0.00%	0.00%

Table 14.2.1 On a scale of 1-5 with "1" as very important and "5" as unimportant, please specify how critical is the office of career services?

	No Answer	Very Important	Important	Somewhat Important	Infrequently Important	Not Really Important
Entire sample	4.76%	19.05%	50.00%	16.67%	7.14%	2.38%

Table 14.2.2 On a scale of 1-5 with "1" as very important and "5" as unimportant, please specify how critical is the office of career services? Broken out for public and private colleges

Your college is:	No Answer	Very Important	Important	Somewhat Important	Infrequently Important	Not Really Important
A public college	0.00%	28.57%	42.86%	14.29%	9.52%	4.76%
A private college	9.52%	9.52%	57.14%	19.05%	4.76%	0.00%

Table 14.2.3 On a scale of 1-5 with "1" as very important and "5" as unimportant, please specify how critical is the office of career services? Broken out by enrollment

Enrollment	No Answer	Very Important	Important	Somewhat Important	Infrequently Important	Not Really Important
Less than 1000	0.00%	0.00%	75.00%	25.00%	0.00%	0.00%
1000 - 2999	20.00%	10.00%	40.00%	10.00%	20.00%	0.00%
3000 - 7000	0.00%	21.43%	57.14%	14.29%	7.14%	0.00%
More than 7000	0.00%	40.00%	30.00%	20.00%	0.00%	10.00%

Table 14.2.4 On a scale of 1-5 with "1" as very important and "5" as unimportant, please specify how critical is the office of career services? Broken out by college type or Carnegie class

College type or Carnegie class	No Answer	Very Important	Important	Somewhat Important	Infrequently Important	Not Really Important
Carnegie Class 4-year or MA degree granting institution, Community College	5.88%	17.65%	52.94%	14.71%	8.82%	0.00%
Carnegie Class Research universities	0.00%	25.00%	37.50%	25.00%	0.00%	12.50%

Table 14.2.5 On a scale of 1-5 with "1" as very important and "5" as unimportant, please specify how critical is the office of career services? Broken out by tuition, $

Tuition, $	No Answer	Very Important	Important	Somewhat Important	Infrequently Important	Not Really Important
Less than 10000	0.00%	16.67%	66.67%	8.33%	8.33%	0.00%
10000 - 20999	0.00%	16.67%	33.33%	33.33%	0.00%	16.67%
21000 - 30000	7.69%	23.08%	53.85%	7.69%	7.69%	0.00%
More than 30000	9.09%	18.18%	36.36%	27.27%	9.09%	0.00%

Table 14.3.1 On a scale of 1-5 with "1" as very important and "5" as unimportant, please specify how critical is the office of academic advising?

	No Answer	Very Important	Important	Somewhat Important	Infrequently Important	Not Really Important
Entire sample	2.38%	71.43%	21.43%	4.76%	0.00%	0.00%

Table 14.3.2 On a scale of 1-5 with "1" as very important and "5" as unimportant, please specify how critical is the office of academic advising? Broken out for public and private colleges

Your college is:	No Answer	Very Important	Important	Somewhat Important	Infrequently Important	Not Really Important
A public college	0.00%	80.95%	14.29%	4.76%	0.00%	0.00%
A private college	4.76%	61.90%	28.57%	4.76%	0.00%	0.00%

Table 14.3.3 On a scale of 1-5 with "1" as very important and "5" as unimportant, please specify how critical is the office of academic advising? Broken out by enrollment

Enrollment	No Answer	Very Important	Important	Somewhat Important	Infrequently Important	Not Really Important
Less than 1000	0.00%	62.50%	37.50%	0.00%	0.00%	0.00%
1000 - 2999	10.00%	60.00%	30.00%	0.00%	0.00%	0.00%
3000 - 7000	0.00%	71.43%	21.43%	7.14%	0.00%	0.00%
More than 7000	0.00%	90.00%	0.00%	10.00%	0.00%	0.00%

Table 14.3.4 On a scale of 1-5 with "1" as very important and "5" as unimportant, please specify how critical is the office of academic advising? Broken out by college type or Carnegie class

College type or Carnegie class	No Answer	Very Important	Important	Somewhat Important	Infrequently Important	Not Really Important
Carnegie Class 4-year or MA degree granting institution, Community College	2.94%	67.65%	26.47%	2.94%	0.00%	0.00%
Carnegie Class Research universities	0.00%	87.50%	0.00%	12.50%	0.00%	0.00%

Table 14.3.5 On a scale of 1-5 with "1" as very important and "5" as unimportant, please specify how critical is the office of academic advising? Broken out by tuition, $

Tuition, $	No Answer	Very Important	Important	Somewhat Important	Infrequently Important	Not Really Important
Less than 10000	0.00%	75.00%	25.00%	0.00%	0.00%	0.00%
10000 - 20999	0.00%	83.33%	0.00%	16.67%	0.00%	0.00%
21000 - 30000	0.00%	61.54%	30.77%	7.69%	0.00%	0.00%
More than 30000	9.09%	72.73%	18.18%	0.00%	0.00%	0.00%

Table 14.4.1 On a scale of 1-5 with "1" as very important and "5" as unimportant, please specify how critical is learning services/tutoring services?

	No Answer	Very Important	Important	Somewhat Important	Infrequently Important	Not Really Important
Entire sample	2.38%	64.29%	21.43%	11.90%	0.00%	0.00%

Table 14.4.2 On a scale of 1-5 with "1" as very important and "5" as unimportant, please specify how critical is learning services/tutoring services? Broken out for public and private colleges

Your college is:	No Answer	Very Important	Important	Somewhat Important	Infrequently Important	Not Really Important
A public college	0.00%	66.67%	23.81%	9.52%	0.00%	0.00%
A private college	4.76%	61.90%	19.05%	14.29%	0.00%	0.00%

Table 14.4.3 On a scale of 1-5 with "1" as very important and "5" as unimportant, please specify how critical is learning services/tutoring services? Broken out by enrollment

Enrollment	No Answer	Very Important	Important	Somewhat Important	Infrequently Important	Not Really Important
Less than 1000	0.00%	50.00%	37.50%	12.50%	0.00%	0.00%
1000 - 2999	10.00%	80.00%	0.00%	10.00%	0.00%	0.00%
3000 - 7000	0.00%	42.86%	42.86%	14.29%	0.00%	0.00%
More than 7000	0.00%	90.00%	0.00%	10.00%	0.00%	0.00%

Table 14.4.4 On a scale of 1-5 with "1" as very important and "5" as unimportant, please specify how critical is learning services/tutoring services? Broken out by college type or Carnegie class

College type or Carnegie class	No Answer	Very Important	Important	Somewhat Important	Infrequently Important	Not Really Important
Carnegie Class 4-year or MA degree granting institution, Community College	2.94%	58.82%	26.47%	11.76%	0.00%	0.00%
Carnegie Class Research universities	0.00%	87.50%	0.00%	12.50%	0.00%	0.00%

Table 14.4.5 On a scale of 1-5 with "1" as very important and "5" as unimportant, please specify how critical is learning services/tutoring services? Broken out by tuition, $

Tuition, $	No Answer	Very Important	Important	Somewhat Important	Infrequently Important	Not Really Important
Less than 10000	0.00%	66.67%	33.33%	0.00%	0.00%	0.00%
10000 - 20999	0.00%	50.00%	16.67%	33.33%	0.00%	0.00%
21000 - 30000	0.00%	69.23%	7.69%	23.08%	0.00%	0.00%
More than 30000	9.09%	63.64%	27.27%	0.00%	0.00%	0.00%

Table 14.5.1 On a scale of 1-5 with "1" as very important and "5" as unimportant, please specify how critical is peer mentoring?

	No Answer	Very Important	Important	Somewhat Important	Infrequently Important	Not Really Important
Entire sample	2.38%	30.95%	40.48%	23.81%	2.38%	0.00%

Table 14.5.2 On a scale of 1-5 with "1" as very important and "5" as unimportant, please specify how critical is peer mentoring? Broken out for public and private colleges

Your college is:	No Answer	Very Important	Important	Somewhat Important	Infrequently Important	Not Really Important
A public college	0.00%	19.05%	47.62%	28.57%	4.76%	0.00%
A private college	4.76%	42.86%	33.33%	19.05%	0.00%	0.00%

Table 14.5.3 On a scale of 1-5 with "1" as very important and "5" as unimportant, please specify how critical is peer mentoring? Broken out by enrollment

Enrollment	No Answer	Very Important	Important	Somewhat Important	Infrequently Important	Not Really Important
Less than 1000	0.00%	37.50%	50.00%	12.50%	0.00%	0.00%
1000 - 2999	10.00%	40.00%	20.00%	30.00%	0.00%	0.00%
3000 - 7000	0.00%	21.43%	50.00%	21.43%	7.14%	0.00%
More than 7000	0.00%	30.00%	40.00%	30.00%	0.00%	0.00%

Table 14.5.4 On a scale of 1-5 with "1" as very important and "5" as unimportant, please specify how critical is peer mentoring? Broken out by college type or Carnegie class

	No Answer	Very Important	Important	Somewhat Important	Infrequently Important	Not Really Important
Carnegie Class 4-year or MA degree granting institution, Community College	2.94%	29.41%	44.12%	20.59%	2.94%	0.00%
Carnegie Class Research universities	0.00%	37.50%	25.00%	37.50%	0.00%	0.00%

Table 14.5.5 On a scale of 1-5 with "1" as very important and "5" as unimportant, please specify how critical is peer mentoring? Broken out by tuition, $

Tuition, $	No Answer	Very Important	Important	Somewhat Important	Infrequently Important	Not Really Important
Less than 10000	0.00%	16.67%	58.33%	25.00%	0.00%	0.00%
10000 - 20999	0.00%	0.00%	66.67%	16.67%	16.67%	0.00%
21000 - 30000	0.00%	38.46%	30.77%	30.77%	0.00%	0.00%
More than 30000	9.09%	54.55%	18.18%	18.18%	0.00%	0.00%

Table 14.6.1 On a scale of 1-5 with "1" as very important and "5" as unimportant, please specify how critical is childcare services?

	No Answer	Very Important	Important	Somewhat Important	Infrequently Important	Not Really Important
Entire sample	7.14%	9.52%	19.05%	30.95%	9.52%	23.81%

Table 14.6.2 On a scale of 1-5 with "1" as very important and "5" as unimportant, please specify how critical is childcare services? Broken out for public and private colleges

Your college is:	No Answer	Very Important	Important	Somewhat Important	Infrequently Important	Not Really Important
A public college	4.76%	14.29%	33.33%	38.10%	4.76%	4.76%
A private college	9.52%	4.76%	4.76%	23.81%	14.29%	42.86%

Table 14.6.3 On a scale of 1-5 with "1" as very important and "5" as unimportant, please specify how critical is childcare services? Broken out by enrollment

Enrollment	No Answer	Very Important	Important	Somewhat Important	Infrequently Important	Not Really Important
Less than 1000	0.00%	12.50%	0.00%	25.00%	25.00%	37.50%
1000 - 2999	20.00%	0.00%	20.00%	20.00%	0.00%	40.00%
3000 - 7000	7.14%	7.14%	28.57%	35.71%	14.29%	7.14%
More than 7000	0.00%	20.00%	20.00%	40.00%	0.00%	20.00%

Table 14.6.4 On a scale of 1-5 with "1" as very important and "5" as unimportant, please specify how critical is childcare services? Broken out by college type or Carnegie class

College type or Carnegie class	No Answer	Very Important	Important	Somewhat Important	Infrequently Important	Not Really Important
Carnegie Class 4-year or MA degree granting institution, Community College	8.82%	5.88%	23.53%	29.41%	11.76%	20.59%
Carnegie Class Research universities	0.00%	25.00%	0.00%	37.50%	0.00%	37.50%

Table 14.6.5 On a scale of 1-5 with "1" as very important and "5" as unimportant, please specify how critical is childcare services? Broken out by tuition, $

Tuition, $	No Answer	Very Important	Important	Somewhat Important	Infrequently Important	Not Really Important
Less than 10000	0.00%	8.33%	41.67%	41.67%	0.00%	8.33%
10000 - 20999	0.00%	0.00%	33.33%	50.00%	16.67%	0.00%
21000 - 30000	15.38%	15.38%	7.69%	23.08%	15.38%	23.08%
More than 30000	9.09%	9.09%	0.00%	18.18%	9.09%	54.55%

Table 14.7.1 On a scale of 1-5 with "1" as very important and "5" as unimportant, please specify how critical is the information technology?

	No Answer	Very Important	Important	Somewhat Important	Infrequently Important	Not Really Important
Entire sample	2.38%	19.05%	38.10%	28.57%	9.52%	2.38%

Table 14.7.2 On a scale of 1-5 with "1" as very important and "5" as unimportant, please specify how critical is the information technology? Broken out for public and private colleges

Your college is:	No Answer	Very Important	Important	Somewhat Important	Infrequently Important	Not Really Important
A public college	0.00%	28.57%	38.10%	23.81%	4.76%	4.76%
A private college	4.76%	9.52%	38.10%	33.33%	14.29%	0.00%

Table 14.7.3 On a scale of 1-5 with "1" as very important and "5" as unimportant, please specify how critical is the information technology? Broken out by enrollment

Enrollment	No Answer	Very Important	Important	Somewhat Important	Infrequently Important	Not Really Important
Less than 1000	0.00%	25.00%	50.00%	12.50%	12.50%	0.00%
1000 - 2999	10.00%	20.00%	30.00%	20.00%	10.00%	10.00%
3000 - 7000	0.00%	21.43%	28.57%	42.86%	7.14%	0.00%
More than 7000	0.00%	10.00%	50.00%	30.00%	10.00%	0.00%

Table 14.7.4 On a scale of 1-5 with "1" as very important and "5" as unimportant, please specify how critical is the information technology? Broken out by college type or Carnegie class

College type or Carnegie class	No Answer	Very Important	Important	Somewhat Important	Infrequently Important	Not Really Important
Carnegie Class 4-year or MA degree granting institution, Community College	2.94%	20.59%	41.18%	23.53%	8.82%	2.94%
Carnegie Class Research universities	0.00%	12.50%	25.00%	50.00%	12.50%	0.00%

Table 14.7.5 On a scale of 1-5 with "1" as very important and "5" as unimportant, please specify how critical is the information technology? Broken out by tuition, $

Tuition, $	No Answer	Very Important	Important	Somewhat Important	Infrequently Important	Not Really Important
Less than 10000	0.00%	33.33%	41.67%	25.00%	0.00%	0.00%
10000 - 20999	0.00%	0.00%	50.00%	33.33%	16.67%	0.00%
21000 - 30000	0.00%	23.08%	46.15%	7.69%	15.38%	7.69%
More than 30000	9.09%	9.09%	18.18%	54.55%	9.09%	0.00%

Table 15.1 Does the college identify high risk students and then intervene at certain thresh-holds such as number of classes or assignments missed, or low grade point averages?

	No Answer	Yes	No
Entire sample	2.38%	85.71%	11.90%

Table 15.2 Does the college identify high risk students and then intervene at certain thresh-holds such as number of classes or assignments missed, or low grade point averages? Broken out for public and private colleges

Your college is:	No Answer	Yes	No
A public college	0.00%	80.95%	19.05%
A private college	4.76%	90.48%	4.76%

Table 15.3 Does the college identify high risk students and then intervene at certain thresh-holds such as number of classes or assignments missed, or low grade point averages? Broken out by enrollment

Enrollment	No Answer	Yes	No
Less than 1000	0.00%	100.00%	0.00%
1000 - 2999	10.00%	90.00%	0.00%
3000 - 7000	0.00%	64.29%	35.71%
More than 7000	0.00%	100.00%	0.00%

Table 15.4 Does the college identify high risk students and then intervene at certain thresh-holds such as number of classes or assignments missed, or low grade point averages? Broken out by college type or Carnegie class

College type or Carnegie class	No Answer	Yes	No
Carnegie Class 4-year or MA degree granting institution, Community College	2.94%	82.35%	14.71%
Carnegie Class Research universities	0.00%	100.00%	0.00%

Table 15.5 Does the college identify high risk students and then intervene at certain thresh-holds such as number of classes or assignments missed, or low grade point averages? Broken out by tuition, $

Tuition, $	No Answer	Yes	No
Less than 10000	0.00%	83.33%	16.67%
10000 - 20999	0.00%	83.33%	16.67%
21000 - 30000	0.00%	92.31%	7.69%
More than 30000	9.09%	81.82%	9.09%

Table 16.1 Which phrase best describes your view of your college's efforts to reach out to and help students at high risk for dropping out?

	No Answer	We don't do enough and are not really very good at what we do.	We don't do enough and our present efforts are passable at best.	We make a fairly considerable effort and do as well as most.	We make a great effort but without great results.	We make a great effort and we have very good results.
Entire sample	2.38%	11.90%	11.90%	40.48%	21.43%	11.90%

Table 16.2 Which phrase best describes your view of your college's efforts to reach out to and help students at high risk for dropping out? Broken out for public and private colleges

Your college is:	No Answer	We don't do enough and are not really very good at what we do.	We don't do enough and our present efforts are passable at best.	We make a fairly considerable effort and do as well as most.	We make a great effort but without great results.	We make a great effort and we have very good results.
A public college	0.00%	14.29%	9.52%	42.86%	23.81%	9.52%
A private college	4.76%	9.52%	14.29%	38.10%	19.05%	14.29%

Table 16.3 Which phrase best describes your view of your college's efforts to reach out to and help students at high risk for dropping out? Broken out by enrollment

Enrollment	No Answer	We don't do enough and are not really very good at what we do.	We don't do enough and our present efforts are passable at best.	We make a fairly considerable effort and do as well as most.	We make a great effort but without great results.	We make a great effort and we have very good results.
Less than 1000	0.00%	12.50%	12.50%	50.00%	25.00%	0.00%
1000 - 2999	10.00%	10.00%	20.00%	20.00%	20.00%	20.00%
3000 - 7000	0.00%	7.14%	7.14%	57.14%	21.43%	7.14%
More than 7000	0.00%	20.00%	10.00%	30.00%	20.00%	20.00%

Table 16.4 Which phrase best describes your view of your college's efforts to reach out to and help students at high risk for dropping out? Broken out by college type or Carnegie class

College type or Carnegie class	No Answer	We don't do enough and are not really very good at what we do.	We don't do enough and our present efforts are passable at best.	We make a fairly considerable effort and do as well as most.	We make a great effort but without great results.	We make a great effort and we have very good results.
Carnegie Class 4-year or MA degree granting institution, Community College	2.94%	11.76%	11.76%	44.12%	20.59%	8.82%
Carnegie Class Research universities	0.00%	12.50%	12.50%	25.00%	25.00%	25.00%

Table 16.5 Which phrase best describes your view of your college's efforts to reach out to and help students at high risk for dropping out? Broken out by tuition, $

Tuition, $	No Answer	We don't do enough and are not really very good at what we do.	We don't do enough and our present efforts are passable at best.	We make a fairly considerable effort and do as well as most.	We make a great effort but without great results.	We make a great effort and we have very good results.
Less than 10000	0.00%	8.33%	16.67%	58.33%	8.33%	8.33%
10000 - 20999	0.00%	33.33%	0.00%	33.33%	16.67%	16.67%
21000 - 30000	0.00%	15.38%	23.08%	23.08%	38.46%	0.00%
More than 30000	9.09%	0.00%	0.00%	45.45%	18.18%	27.27%

Table 17 What is the college spending (in US $) on tutoring for all students?

Table 17.1.1 How much did the college spend (in US $) on tutoring for all students in the past year?

	Mean	Median	Minimum	Maximum
Entire sample	78480.00	44000.00	5000.00	550000.00

Table 17.1.2 How much did the college spend (in US $) on tutoring for all students in the past year? Broken out for public and private colleges

Your college is:	Mean	Median	Minimum	Maximum
A public college	39760.00	25000.00	5000.00	100000.00
A private college	117200.00	57500.00	9000.00	550000.00

Table 17.1.3 How much did the college spend (in US $) on tutoring for all students in the past year? Broken out by enrollment

Enrollment	Mean	Median	Minimum	Maximum
Less than 1000	39400.00	38000.00	9000.00	75000.00
1000 - 2999	31520.00	25000.00	12600.00	65000.00
3000 - 7000	45000.00	47500.00	5000.00	80000.00
More than 7000	172500.00	87500.00	10000.00	550000.00

Table 17.1.4 How much did the college spend (in US $) on tutoring for all students in the past year? Broken out by college type or Carnegie class

College type or Carnegie class	Mean	Median	Minimum	Maximum
Carnegie Class 4-year or MA degree granting institution, Community College	41225.00	34000.00	5000.00	80000.00
Carnegie Class Research universities	227500.00	175000.00	10000.00	550000.00

Table 17.1.5 How much did the college spend (in US $) on tutoring for all students in the past year? Broken out by tuition, $

Tuition, $	Mean	Median	Minimum	Maximum
Less than 10000	25000.00	25000.00	5000.00	50000.00
10000 - 20999	87500.00	87500.00	75000.00	100000.00
21000 - 30000	30942.86	25000.00	9000.00	80000.00
More than 30000	175500.00	75000.00	38000.00	550000.00

Table 17.2.1 How much will the college spend (in US $) next year on tutoring for all students?

	Mean	Median	Minimum	Maximum
Entire sample	80280.00	45000.00	5000.00	562000.00

Table 17.2.2 How much will the college spend (in US $) next year on tutoring for all students? Broken out for public and private colleges

Your college is:	Mean	Median	Minimum	Maximum
A public college	41160.00	32000.00	5000.00	100000.00
A private college	119400.00	57500.00	9000.00	562000.00

Table 17.2.3 How much will the college spend (in US $) next year on tutoring for all students? Broken out by enrollment

Enrollment	Mean	Median	Minimum	Maximum
Less than 1000	39400.00	38000.00	9000.00	75000.00
1000 - 2999	36320.00	39000.00	12600.00	65000.00
3000 - 7000	45000.00	47500.00	5000.00	80000.00
More than 7000	174500.00	87500.00	10000.00	562000.00

Table 17.2.4 How much will the college spend (in US $) next year on tutoring for all students? Broken out by college type or Carnegie class

College type or Carnegie class	Mean	Median	Minimum	Maximum
Carnegie Class 4-year or MA degree granting institution, Community College	42725.00	39500.00	5000.00	80000.00
Carnegie Class Research universities	230500.00	175000.00	10000.00	562000.00

Table 17.2.5 How much will the college spend (in US $) next year on tutoring for all students? Broken out by tuition, $

Tuition, $	Mean	Median	Minimum	Maximum
Less than 10000	27800.00	25000.00	5000.00	50000.00
10000 - 20999	87500.00	87500.00	75000.00	100000.00
21000 - 30000	32371.43	25000.00	9000.00	80000.00
More than 30000	177500.00	75000.00	38000.00	562000.00

Table 18.1 Which phrase best describes your attitude towards the impact that the college tutoring program has had on student retention?

	No Answer	I don't think that tutoring can have a big impact on retention.	We need to hire more tutors, train them better, or both.	We have a good tutoring program that has helped us to maintain or increase our retention levels.	Our tutoring program is excellent and is a key factor in our maintenance of a higher than expected retention level.
Entire sample	9.52%	2.38%	40.48%	40.48%	7.14%

Table 18.2 Which phrase best describes your attitude towards the impact that the college tutoring program has had on student retention? Broken out for public and private colleges

Your college is:	No Answer	I don't think that tutoring can have a big impact on retention.	We need to hire more tutors, train them better, or both.	We have a good tutoring program that has helped us to maintain or increase our retention levels.	Our tutoring program is excellent and is a key factor in our maintenance of a higher than expected retention level.
A public college	9.52%	0.00%	47.62%	33.33%	9.52%
A private college	9.52%	4.76%	33.33%	47.62%	4.76%

Table 18.3 Which phrase best describes your attitude towards the impact that the college tutoring program has had on student retention? Broken out by enrollment

Enrollment	No Answer	I don't think that tutoring can have a big impact on retention.	We need to hire more tutors, train them better, or both.	We have a good tutoring program that has helped us to maintain or increase our retention levels.	Our tutoring program is excellent and is a key factor in our maintenance of a higher than expected retention level.
Less than 1000	12.50%	0.00%	50.00%	37.50%	0.00%
1000 - 2999	10.00%	10.00%	30.00%	40.00%	10.00%
3000 - 7000	0.00%	0.00%	50.00%	42.86%	7.14%
More than 7000	20.00%	0.00%	30.00%	40.00%	10.00%

Table 18.4 Which phrase best describes your attitude towards the impact that the college tutoring program has had on student retention? Broken out by college type or Carnegie class

College type or Carnegie class	No Answer	I don't think that tutoring can have a big impact on retention.	We need to hire more tutors, train them better, or both.	We have a good tutoring program that has helped us to maintain or increase our retention levels.	Our tutoring program is excellent and is a key factor in our maintenance of a higher than expected retention level.
Carnegie Class 4-year or MA degree granting institution, Community College	5.88%	2.94%	47.06%	35.29%	8.82%
Carnegie Class Research universities	25.00%	0.00%	12.50%	62.50%	0.00%

Table 18.5 Which phrase best describes your attitude towards the impact that the college tutoring program has had on student retention? Broken out by tuition, $

Tuition, $	No Answer	I don't think that tutoring can have a big impact on retention.	We need to hire more tutors, train them better, or both.	We have a good tutoring program that has helped us to maintain or increase our retention levels.	Our tutoring program is excellent and is a key factor in our maintenance of a higher than expected retention level.
Less than 10000	16.67%	0.00%	33.33%	41.67%	8.33%
10000 - 20999	0.00%	0.00%	50.00%	33.33%	16.67%
21000 - 30000	7.69%	7.69%	61.54%	23.08%	0.00%
More than 30000	9.09%	0.00%	18.18%	63.64%	9.09%

Table 19.1 Does the college have student advisory centers located in residence halls?

	No Answer	Yes	No
Entire sample	9.52%	7.14%	83.33%

Table 19.2 Does the college have student advisory centers located in residence halls? Broken out for public and private colleges

Your college is:	No Answer	Yes	No
A public college	4.76%	9.52%	85.71%
A private college	14.29%	4.76%	80.95%

Table 19.3 Does the college have student advisory centers located in residence halls? Broken out by enrollment

Enrollment	No Answer	Yes	No
Less than 1000	12.50%	0.00%	87.50%
1000 - 2999	10.00%	0.00%	90.00%
3000 - 7000	0.00%	7.14%	92.86%
More than 7000	20.00%	20.00%	60.00%

Table 19.4 Does the college have student advisory centers located in residence halls? Broken out by college type or Carnegie class

College type or Carnegie class	No Answer	Yes	No
Carnegie Class 4-year or MA degree granting institution, Community College	5.88%	5.88%	88.24%
Carnegie Class Research universities	25.00%	12.50%	62.50%

Table 19.5 Does the college have student advisory centers located in residence halls? Broken out by tuition, $

Tuition, $	No Answer	Yes	No
Less than 10000	8.33%	16.67%	75.00%
10000 - 20999	0.00%	0.00%	100.00%
21000 - 30000	7.69%	0.00%	92.31%
More than 30000	18.18%	9.09%	72.73%

Table 20.1 To the best of your knowledge, has the college ever hired a consultant to review or advise on the college's academic advising services?

	No Answer	Yes	No
Entire sample	11.90%	23.81%	64.29%

Table 20.2 To the best of your knowledge, has the college ever hired a consultant to review or advise on the college's academic advising services? Broken out for public and private colleges

Your college is:	No Answer	Yes	No
A public college	9.52%	33.33%	57.14%
A private college	14.29%	14.29%	71.43%

Table 20.3 To the best of your knowledge, has the college ever hired a consultant to review or advise on the college's academic advising services? Broken out by enrollment

Enrollment	No Answer	Yes	No
Less than 1000	12.50%	0.00%	87.50%
1000 - 2999	20.00%	10.00%	70.00%
3000 - 7000	0.00%	21.43%	78.57%
More than 7000	20.00%	60.00%	20.00%

Table 20.4 To the best of your knowledge, has the college ever hired a consultant to review or advise on the college's academic advising services? Broken out by college type or Carnegie class

College type or Carnegie class	No Answer	Yes	No
Carnegie Class 4-year or MA degree granting institution, Community College	8.82%	17.65%	73.53%
Carnegie Class Research universities	25.00%	50.00%	25.00%

Table 20.5 To the best of your knowledge, has the college ever hired a consultant to review or advise on the college's academic advising services? Broken out by tuition, $

Tuition, $	No Answer	Yes	No
Less than 10000	16.67%	33.33%	50.00%
10000 - 20999	0.00%	33.33%	66.67%
21000 - 30000	7.69%	7.69%	84.62%
More than 30000	18.18%	27.27%	54.55%

Table 21.1 What is the total annual budget (in US $), including spending for salaries, of the college's academic advising unit?

	Mean	Median	Minimum	Maximum
Entire sample	577700.41	245000.00	0.00	3000000.00

Table 21.2 What is the total annual budget (in US $), including spending for salaries, of the college's academic advising unit? Broken out for public and private colleges

Your college is:	Mean	Median	Minimum	Maximum
A public college	414113.38	371358.50	75000.00	1200000.00
A private college	723111.11	163000.00	0.00	3000000.00

Table 21.3 What is the total annual budget (in US $), including spending for salaries, of the college's academic advising unit? Broken out by enrollment

Enrollment	Mean	Median	Minimum	Maximum
Less than 1000	171000.00	163000.00	100000.00	250000.00
1000 - 2999	151428.57	100000.00	0.00	400000.00
3000 - 7000	300905.67	342717.00	160000.00	400000.00
More than 7000	1836297.50	1850000.00	645190.00	3000000.00

Table 21.4 What is the total annual budget (in US $), including spending for salaries, of the college's academic advising unit? Broken out by college type or Carnegie class

College type or Carnegie class	Mean	Median	Minimum	Maximum
Carnegie Class 4-year or MA degree granting institution, Community College	291136.21	161500.00	0.00	1200000.00
Carnegie Class Research universities	1915000.00	2500000.00	245000.00	3000000.00

Table 21.5 What is the total annual budget (in US $), including spending for salaries, of the college's academic advising unit? Broken out by tuition, $

Tuition, $	Mean	Median	Minimum	Maximum
Less than 10000	483543.40	400000.00	75000.00	1200000.00
10000 - 20999	645190.00	645190.00	645190.00	645190.00
21000 - 30000	135500.00	155000.00	0.00	250000.00
More than 30000	1189000.00	245000.00	100000.00	3000000.00

Table 22.1 Over the past two years the college's financial aid has become more or less generous?

	No Answer	Become much less generous	Become somewhat less generous	Remained about the same in real terms	Become somewhat more generous	Become much more generous
Entire sample	7.14%	4.76%	7.14%	50.00%	30.95%	0.00%

Table 22.2 Over the past two years the college's financial aid has become more or less generous? Broken out for public and private colleges

Your college is:	No Answer	Become much less generous	Become somewhat less generous	Remained about the same in real terms	Become somewhat more generous	Become much more generous
A public college	4.76%	4.76%	9.52%	57.14%	23.81%	0.00%
A private college	9.52%	4.76%	4.76%	42.86%	38.10%	0.00%

Table 22.3 Over the past two years the college's financial aid has become more or less generous? Broken out by enrollment

Enrollment	No Answer	Become much less generous	Become somewhat less generous	Remained about the same in real terms	Become somewhat more generous	Become much more generous
Less than 1000	0.00%	12.50%	12.50%	50.00%	25.00%	0.00%
1000 - 2999	10.00%	0.00%	0.00%	60.00%	30.00%	0.00%
3000 - 7000	0.00%	0.00%	7.14%	64.29%	28.57%	0.00%
More than 7000	20.00%	10.00%	10.00%	20.00%	40.00%	0.00%

Table 22.4 Over the past two years the college's financial aid has become more or less generous? Broken out by college type or Carnegie class

College type or Carnegie class	No Answer	Become much less generous	Become somewhat less generous	Remained about the same in real terms	Become somewhat more generous	Become much more generous
Carnegie Class 4-year or MA degree granting institution, Community College	2.94%	2.94%	8.82%	55.88%	29.41%	0.00%
Carnegie Class Research universities	25.00%	12.50%	0.00%	25.00%	37.50%	0.00%

Table 22.5 Over the past two years the college's financial aid has become more or less generous? Broken out by tuition, $

Tuition, $	No Answer	Become much less generous	Become somewhat less generous	Remained about the same in real terms	Become somewhat more generous	Become much more generous
Less than 10000	8.33%	0.00%	8.33%	66.67%	16.67%	0.00%
10000 - 20999	0.00%	0.00%	16.67%	33.33%	50.00%	0.00%
21000 - 30000	0.00%	15.38%	0.00%	76.92%	7.69%	0.00%
More than 30000	18.18%	0.00%	9.09%	9.09%	63.64%	0.00%

Table 23.1 My personal feeling about tuition levels and the financial situation of our student body is that:

	No Answer	It has become more and more difficult for our students to pay for college.	The overall financial burden on our students has not changed much in recent years.	Our aid programs and a strong economy have actually reduced the financial burden on our students in recent years.
Entire sample	7.14%	52.38%	33.33%	7.14%

Table 23.2 My personal feeling about tuition levels and the financial situation of our student body is that: Broken out for public and private colleges

Your college is:	No Answer	It has become more and more difficult for our students to pay for college.	The overall financial burden on our students has not changed much in recent years.	Our aid programs and a strong economy have actually reduced the financial burden on our students in recent years.
A public college	4.76%	61.90%	33.33%	0.00%
A private college	9.52%	42.86%	33.33%	14.29%

Table 23.3 My personal feeling about tuition levels and the financial situation of our student body is that: Broken out by enrollment

Enrollment	No Answer	It has become more and more difficult for our students to pay for college.	The overall financial burden on our students has not changed much in recent years.	Our aid programs and a strong economy have actually reduced the financial burden on our students in recent years.
Less than 1000	0.00%	62.50%	25.00%	12.50%
1000 - 2999	10.00%	50.00%	30.00%	10.00%
3000 - 7000	0.00%	50.00%	50.00%	0.00%
More than 7000	20.00%	50.00%	20.00%	10.00%

Table 23.4 My personal feeling about tuition levels and the financial situation of our student body is that: Broken out by college type or Carnegie class

College type or Carnegie class	No Answer	It has become more and more difficult for our students to pay for college.	The overall financial burden on our students has not changed much in recent years.	Our aid programs and a strong economy have actually reduced the financial burden on our students in recent years.
Carnegie Class 4-year or MA degree granting institution, Community College	2.94%	55.88%	35.29%	5.88%
Carnegie Class Research universities	25.00%	37.50%	25.00%	12.50%

able 23.5 My personal feeling about tuition levels and the financial situation of our student body is that: Broken out by tuition, $

Tuition, $	No Answer	It has become more and more difficult for our students to pay for college.	The overall financial burden on our students has not changed much in recent years.	Our aid programs and a strong economy have actually reduced the financial burden on our students in recent years.
Less than 10000	8.33%	50.00%	41.67%	0.00%
10000 - 20999	0.00%	83.33%	0.00%	16.67%
21000 - 30000	0.00%	46.15%	53.85%	0.00%
More than 30000	18.18%	45.45%	18.18%	18.18%

Table 24.1 The college's retention rate for first year students entering the second year has increased, decreased or remained the same?

	No Answer	Remained about the same in the past two years	Increased in the past two years	Decreased in the past two years
Entire sample	7.14%	52.38%	23.81%	16.67%

Table 24.2 The college's retention rate for first year students entering the second year has increased, decreased or remained the same? Broken out for public and private colleges

Your college is:	No Answer	Remained about the same in the past two years	Increased in the past two years	Decreased in the past two years
A public college	4.76%	57.14%	19.05%	19.05%
A private college	9.52%	47.62%	28.57%	14.29%

Table 24.3 The college's retention rate for first year students entering the second year has increased, decreased or remained the same? Broken out by enrollment

Enrollment	No Answer	Remained about the same in the past two years	Increased in the past two years	Decreased in the past two years
Less than 1000	0.00%	37.50%	37.50%	25.00%
1000 - 2999	10.00%	50.00%	30.00%	10.00%
3000 - 7000	7.14%	57.14%	21.43%	14.29%
More than 7000	10.00%	60.00%	10.00%	20.00%

Table 24.4 The college's retention rate for first year students entering the second year has increased, decreased or remained the same? Broken out by college type or Carnegie class

College type or Carnegie class	No Answer	Remained about the same in the past two years	Increased in the past two years	Decreased in the past two years
Carnegie Class 4-year or MA degree granting institution, Community College	5.88%	50.00%	26.47%	17.65%
Carnegie Class Research universities	12.50%	62.50%	12.50%	12.50%

Table 24.5 The college's retention rate for first year students entering the second year has increased, decreased or remained the same? Broken out by tuition, $

Tuition, $	No Answer	Remained about the same in the past two years	Increased in the past two years	Decreased in the past two years
Less than 10000	8.33%	50.00%	33.33%	8.33%
10000 - 20999	0.00%	33.33%	0.00%	66.67%
21000 - 30000	0.00%	61.54%	23.08%	15.38%
More than 30000	18.18%	54.55%	27.27%	0.00%

Table 25.1 About what percentage of students who drop out do you believe do so primarily for economic reasons?

	Mean	Median	Minimum	Maximum
Entire sample	41.53	35.00	10.00	90.00

Table 25.2 About what percentage of students who drop out do you believe do so primarily for economic reasons? Broken out for public and private colleges

Your college is:	Mean	Median	Minimum	Maximum
A public college	42.75	31.00	10.00	90.00
A private college	40.23	40.00	15.00	85.00

Table 25.3 About what percentage of students who drop out do you believe do so primarily for economic reasons? Broken out by enrollment

Enrollment	Mean	Median	Minimum	Maximum
Less than 1000	51.83	55.00	15.00	85.00
1000 - 2999	36.36	35.00	15.00	65.00
3000 - 7000	37.00	30.00	10.00	90.00
More than 7000	45.00	30.00	20.00	90.00

Table 25.4 About what percentage of students who drop out do you believe do so primarily for economic reasons? Broken out by college type or Carnegie class

College type or Carnegie class	Mean	Median	Minimum	Maximum
Carnegie Class 4-year or MA degree granting institution, Community College	40.10	33.50	10.00	90.00
Carnegie Class Research universities	49.00	50.00	20.00	90.00

Table 25.5 About what percentage of students who drop out do you believe do so primarily for economic reasons? Broken out by tuition, $

Tuition, $	Mean	Median	Minimum	Maximum
Less than 10000	50.22	50.00	15.00	90.00
10000 - 20999	42.00	30.00	10.00	90.00
21000 - 30000	35.55	33.50	15.00	85.00
More than 30000	38.57	25.00	15.00	85.00

Table 26.1 Over the next few years your best honest estimate is that retention rates will decline, stay the same or increase?

	No Answer	Our retention rates will probably decline.	Our retention rates will probably stay about the same.	Our retention rates will increase.
Entire sample	7.14%	4.76%	54.76%	33.33%

Table 26.2 Over the next few years your best honest estimate is that retention rates will decline, stay the same or increase? Broken out for public and private colleges

Your college is:	No Answer	Our retention rates will probably decline.	Our retention rates will probably stay about the same.	Our retention rates will increase.
A public college	4.76%	9.52%	42.86%	42.86%
A private college	9.52%	0.00%	66.67%	23.81%

Table 26.3 Over the next few years your best honest estimate is that retention rates will decline, stay the same or increase? Broken out by enrollment

Enrollment	No Answer	Our retention rates will probably decline.	Our retention rates will probably stay about the same.	Our retention rates will increase.
Less than 1000	0.00%	0.00%	75.00%	25.00%
1000 - 2999	10.00%	0.00%	60.00%	30.00%
3000 - 7000	7.14%	7.14%	35.71%	50.00%
More than 7000	10.00%	10.00%	60.00%	20.00%

Table 26.4 Over the next few years your best honest estimate is that retention rates will decline, stay the same or increase? Broken out by college type or Carnegie class

College type or Carnegie class	No Answer	Our retention rates will probably decline.	Our retention rates will probably stay about the same.	Our retention rates will increase.
Carnegie Class 4-year or MA degree granting institution, Community College	5.88%	5.88%	52.94%	35.29%
Carnegie Class Research universities	12.50%	0.00%	62.50%	25.00%

Table 26.5 Over the next few years your best honest estimate is that retention rates will decline, stay the same or increase? Broken out by tuition, $

Tuition, $	No Answer	Our retention rates will probably decline.	Our retention rates will probably stay about the same.	Our retention rates will increase.
Less than 10000	8.33%	0.00%	50.00%	41.67%
10000 - 20999	0.00%	16.67%	33.33%	50.00%
21000 - 30000	0.00%	7.69%	76.92%	15.38%
More than 30000	18.18%	0.00%	45.45%	36.36%

Table 27 If your college has any of the following types of programs rank their retention rates relative to your main college program

Table 27.1.1 If your college has adult education rank its retention rates relative to your main college program

	No Answer	Retention Rates Much Below Traditional Programs	Retention Rates Below Traditional Programs	About the Same	Above Traditional Programs	Much Above Traditional Programs
Entire sample	64.29%	2.38%	7.14%	14.29%	11.90%	0.00%

Table 27.1.2 If your college has adult education rank its retention rates relative to your main college program Broken out for public and private colleges

Your college is:	No Answer	Retention Rates Much Below Traditional Programs	Retention Rates Below Traditional Programs	About the Same	Above Traditional Programs	Much Above Traditional Programs
A public college	61.90%	4.76%	14.29%	9.52%	9.52%	0.00%
A private college	66.67%	0.00%	0.00%	19.05%	14.29%	0.00%

Table 27.1.3 If your college has adult education rank its retention rates relative to your main college program Broken out by enrollment

Enrollment	No Answer	Retention Rates Much Below Traditional Programs	Retention Rates Below Traditional Programs	About the Same	Above Traditional Programs	Much Above Traditional Programs
Less than 1000	50.00%	0.00%	0.00%	12.50%	37.50%	0.00%
1000 - 2999	90.00%	0.00%	0.00%	10.00%	0.00%	0.00%
3000 - 7000	42.86%	7.14%	14.29%	21.43%	14.29%	0.00%
More than 7000	80.00%	0.00%	10.00%	10.00%	0.00%	0.00%

Table 27.1.4 If your college has adult education rank its retention rates relative to your main college program Broken out by college type or Carnegie class

College type or Carnegie class	No Answer	Retention Rates Much Below Traditional Programs	Retention Rates Below Traditional Programs	About the Same	Above Traditional Programs	Much Above Traditional Programs
Carnegie Class 4-year or MA degree granting institution, Community College	58.82%	2.94%	8.82%	14.71%	14.71%	0.00%
Carnegie Class Research universities	87.50%	0.00%	0.00%	12.50%	0.00%	0.00%

Table 27.1.5 If your college has adult education rank its retention rates relative to your main college program Broken out by tuition, $

Tuition, $	No Answer	Retention Rates Much Below Traditional Programs	Retention Rates Below Traditional Programs	About the Same	Above Traditional Programs	Much Above Traditional Programs
Less than 10000	41.67%	8.33%	25.00%	16.67%	8.33%	0.00%
10000 - 20999	83.33%	0.00%	0.00%	0.00%	16.67%	0.00%
21000 - 30000	76.92%	0.00%	0.00%	15.38%	7.69%	0.00%
More than 30000	63.64%	0.00%	0.00%	18.18%	18.18%	0.00%

Table 27.2.1 If your college has distance education rank its retention rates relative to your main college program

	No Answer	Retention Rates Much Below Traditional Programs	Retention Rates Below Traditional Programs	About the Same	Above Traditional Programs	Much Above Traditional Programs
Entire sample	52.38%	2.38%	11.90%	30.95%	2.38%	0.00%

Table 27.2.2 If your college has distance education rank its retention rates relative to your main college program Broken out for public and private colleges

Your college is:	No Answer	Retention Rates Much Below Traditional Programs	Retention Rates Below Traditional Programs	About the Same	Above Traditional Programs	Much Above Traditional Programs
A public college	42.86%	0.00%	19.05%	38.10%	0.00%	0.00%
A private college	61.90%	4.76%	4.76%	23.81%	4.76%	0.00%

Table 27.2.3 If your college has distance education rank its retention rates relative to your main college program Broken out by enrollment

Enrollment	No Answer	Retention Rates Much Below Traditional Programs	Retention Rates Below Traditional Programs	About the Same	Above Traditional Programs	Much Above Traditional Programs
Less than 1000	62.50%	0.00%	12.50%	12.50%	12.50%	0.00%
1000 - 2999	70.00%	10.00%	10.00%	10.00%	0.00%	0.00%
3000 - 7000	21.43%	0.00%	14.29%	64.29%	0.00%	0.00%
More than 7000	70.00%	0.00%	10.00%	20.00%	0.00%	0.00%

Table 27.2.4 If your college has distance education rank its retention rates relative to your main college program Broken out by college type or Carnegie class

College type or Carnegie class	No Answer	Retention Rates Much Below Traditional Programs	Retention Rates Below Traditional Programs	About the Same	Above Traditional Programs	Much Above Traditional Programs
Carnegie Class 4-year or MA degree granting institution, Community College	47.06%	2.94%	14.71%	32.35%	2.94%	0.00%
Carnegie Class Research universities	75.00%	0.00%	0.00%	25.00%	0.00%	0.00%

Table 27.2.5 If your college has distance education rank its retention rates relative to your main college program Broken out by tuition, $

Tuition, $	No Answer	Retention Rates Much Below Traditional Programs	Retention Rates Below Traditional Programs	About the Same	Above Traditional Programs	Much Above Traditional Programs
Less than 10000	25.00%	0.00%	33.33%	41.67%	0.00%	0.00%
10000 - 20999	66.67%	0.00%	16.67%	16.67%	0.00%	0.00%
21000 - 30000	53.85%	7.69%	0.00%	30.77%	7.69%	0.00%
More than 30000	72.73%	0.00%	0.00%	27.27%	0.00%	0.00%

Table 27.3.1 If your college has an overseas campus rank its retention rates relative to your main college program

	No Answer	Retention Rates Much Below Traditional Programs	Retention Rates Below Traditional Programs	About the Same	Above Traditional Programs	Much Above Traditional Programs
Entire sample	92.86%	0.00%	0.00%	2.38%	2.38%	2.38%

Table 27.3.2 If your college has an overseas campus rank its retention rates relative to your main college program Broken out for public and private colleges

Your college is:	No Answer	Retention Rates Much Below Traditional Programs	Retention Rates Below Traditional Programs	About the Same	Above Traditional Programs	Much Above Traditional Programs
A public college	90.48%	0.00%	0.00%	4.76%	4.76%	0.00%
A private college	95.24%	0.00%	0.00%	0.00%	0.00%	4.76%

Table 27.3.3 If your college has an overseas campus rank its retention rates relative to your main college program Broken out by enrollment

Enrollment	No Answer	Retention Rates Much Below Traditional Programs	Retention Rates Below Traditional Programs	About the Same	Above Traditional Programs	Much Above Traditional Programs
Less than 1000	100.00%	0.00%	0.00%	0.00%	0.00%	0.00%
1000 - 2999	100.00%	0.00%	0.00%	0.00%	0.00%	0.00%
3000 - 7000	85.71%	0.00%	0.00%	7.14%	0.00%	7.14%
More than 7000	90.00%	0.00%	0.00%	0.00%	10.00%	0.00%

Table 27.3.4 If your college has an overseas campus rank their retention rates relative to your main college program Broken out by college type or Carnegie class

College type or Carnegie class	No Answer	Retention Rates Much Below Traditional Programs	Retention Rates Below Traditional Programs	About the Same	Above Traditional Programs	Much Above Traditional Programs
Carnegie Class 4-year or MA degree granting institution, Community College	94.12%	0.00%	0.00%	2.94%	0.00%	2.94%
Carnegie Class Research universities	87.50%	0.00%	0.00%	0.00%	12.50%	0.00%

Table 27.3.5 If your college has an overseas campus rank its retention rates relative to your main college program Broken out by tuition, $

Tuition, $	No Answer	Retention Rates Much Below Traditional Programs	Retention Rates Below Traditional Programs	About the Same	Above Traditional Programs	Much Above Traditional Programs
Less than 10000	91.67%	0.00%	0.00%	8.33%	0.00%	0.00%
10000 - 20999	100.00%	0.00%	0.00%	0.00%	0.00%	0.00%
21000 - 30000	84.62%	0.00%	0.00%	0.00%	7.69%	7.69%
More than 30000	100.00%	0.00%	0.00%	0.00%	0.00%	0.00%

If you have taken any special measures to increase retention in distance learning or adult education programs share with us some or your insights below: Broken out by college type or Carnegie class

Carnegie Class 4-year or MA degree granting institution, Community College

1) more aggressive outreach before the start of the term to alleviate problems before they arise
2) Aside from providing announcements and boosting social media campaigns, we have not done much in this area (to my knowledge).
3) Working to provide more services to adult students in the evening, including expansion of available tutoring. Also working with Student Affairs to make sure that "perks" or "fun" offered to students during day hours are extended to adult students in evening hours.
4) We are just beginning this process
5) NA
6) Currently being assessed.
7) N/A
8) NA
9) improved communication; tried to counter the mixed messages from internal sources
10) unknown

Carnegie Class Research Universities

1) We have done some research in this area but have not taken action yet.
2) NA
3) do not know

86500758R00080